MW00720815

WITH WORKBOOK

TOP NOTCH

English for Today's World

3A

WITH WORKBOOK

TOP NOTCH

English for Today's World

3A

Joan Saslow ■ Allen Ascher

With *Top Notch Pop Songs and Karaoke*
by Rob Morsberger

PEARSON
Longman

Top Notch: English for Today's World   3A with Workbook

Copyright © 2006 by Pearson Education, Inc.
All rights reserved. No part of this publication may be reproduced, stored in a retrieval system, or transmitted in any form or by any means, electronic, mechanical, photocopying, recording, or otherwise, without the prior permission of the publisher.

Pearson Education, 10 Bank Street, White Plains, NY 10606

Editorial director: Pamela Fishman
Senior development editor: Peter Benson
Development editor: Nicole Santos
Vice president, director of design and production: Rhea Banker
Director of electronic production: Aliza Greenblatt
Managing editor: Mike Kemper
Production editors: Marc Oliver, Michael Mone
Art director: Ann France
Senior manufacturing buyer: Dave Dickey
Photo research: Aerin Csigay
Digital layout specialist: Warren Fischbach
Text composition: Kirchoff/Wohlberg, Inc., Word & Image Design Studio, Inc.
Text font: Palatino 11/13, Frutiger 10/12
Cover photograph: "From Above," by Rhea Banker. Copyright © 2005 Rhea Banker.

Text credits: "Beautiful Boy," Words and Music by John Lennon © 1980 LENONO.MUSIC
All Rights Controlled and Administered by EMI BLACKWOOD MUSIC, INC.
All Rights Reserved. International Copyright Secured. Used by Permission.

Photo credits: All original photography by David Mager. Page 2 (Sydney) Peter Adams/Getty Images, (Cambridge) Steve Vidler/SuperStock, (London) Gail M. Shumway/Bruce Coleman, Inc., (Auckland) Rex A. Butcher/Bruce Coleman, Inc., (Edinburgh) Ken Sherman/Bruce Coleman, Inc., (San Francisco) Claver Carroll/PhotoLibrary.com, (Cape Town) Hein von Horsten/Gallo Images/Corbis, (New York) Jochen Tack/Peter Arnold, Inc., (Toronto) SuperStock; p. 5 (middle) Tom & Dee Ann McCarthy/Corbis; p. 7 (top) Russ Lappa, (bottom) Dave King/Dorling Kindersley; p. 9 Will & Deni McIntyre/Getty Images; p. 10 Elpida Memory, Inc.; p. 12 Royalty-Free/Corbis; p. 13 Angelo Cavalli/Getty Images; p. 14 (top) Dorling Kindersley, (left) Bob Daemmrich/The Image Works, (middle) Frozen Images/The Image Works, (right) Adam Woolfitt/Woodfin Camp & Associates; p. 17 Garry Gay/Mira.com; p. 19 (left to right) Will & Deni McIntyre/Photo Researchers, Inc., Maxine Hall/Corbis, Custom Medical Stock Photo, Inc., Lew Lause/SuperStock, Lester Lefkowitz/Corbis; p. 20 (top to bottom) Digital Vision Ltd./SuperStock, Sylvia Johnson/Woodfin Camp & Associates, Phil Schermeister/Corbis, Barbara P. Williams/Bruce Coleman Inc., Charles Gupton/Corbis, Paul Barton/Corbis; p. 22 (ragweed) Getty Images, (bacteria) David Spears/Corbis; p. 23 Royalty-Free/Corbis; p. 26 Arnulf Husmo/Getty Images; p. 29 Getty Images; p. 31 (left to right) Xerox Corporation, George Hall/Corbis, Michael Newman/PhotoEdit, Michelle D. Bridwell/PhotoEdit; p. 34 (caterer) Stewart Cohen/Getty Images, (DJ) Jeff Greenberg/The Image Works; p. 38 (top to bottom) V.O. Press/PhotoEdit, C Squared Studios/Getty Images, Olympus America Inc., Siede Preis/Getty Images, Siede Preis/Getty Images; p. 44 Benelux Press/Index Stock Imagery; p. 45 Steve Gorton/Dorling Kindersley; p. 46 (left) DPA/The Image Works, (right) Bettmann/Corbis; p. 47 (left) Steve Gorton/Dorling Kindersley, (right) Dorling Kindersley; p. 50 (background) Nancy R. Cohen/Getty Images, (top left) Russell Gordon/Odyssey, (top right) Hong Suk-young and Son Kwan-soo, (middle left) Steve Vidler/SuperStock, (middle right) Tony Freeman/PhotoEdit, (bottom left) Stephanie Maze/Woodfin Camp & Associates, (bottom right) AP Wide World Photos; p. 51 John Paul Endress; p. 52 (background) SuperStock, (cake) Michael Newman/PhotoEdit, (fireworks) SuperStock, (parades) Chip East/Corbis, (picnics) Michael Newman/PhotoEdit, (pray) Zafer Kizilkaya/Coral Planet, (gifts) Ryan McVay/Getty Images, (dead) Doug Martin/Photo Researchers, Inc., (costumes) Philip Gould/Corbis; p. 54 Steve Shott/Dorling Kindersley; p. 55 Stephen Hayward/Dorling Kindersley; p. 56 (top) Richard Powers/Corbis, (left) Mark Downey/Lucid Images, (right) Pablo Corral/Corbis; p. 57 Prentice Hall School Division; p. 58 (left) Elyse Lewin/Getty Images, (middle) Stockbyte/SuperStock, (right) Darama/Corbis; p. W1 Lloyd Sutton/Masterfile, (top right) Ron Watts/Corbis, (bottom left) Jean-Marc LaRoque/Auscape International, (bottom right) Sime/eStock Photo; p. W5 AP/Wide World Photos; p. W8 Archivo Iconografico, S.A./Corbis; p. W11 www.CartoonStock.com; p. W14 Corbis; p. W16 Maxine Hall/Corbis, Custom Medical Stock Photo, Inc.; p. W17 Getty Images; p. W37 (top) Helen Atkinson/Reuters/Corbis, (bottom) The Galerie St. Etienne; p. W46 John Paul Endress; p. W49 David Michael Zimmerman/Corbis; p. W51 (left) Stockbyte, (right) Comstock/Getty Images; p. W55 Roy Ooms/Masterfile.

Illustration credits: Steve Attoe, pp. 28, W22, W26; Leanne Franson, p. W50 (bottom); Chris Gash, p. 61; Brian Hughes, pp. 27, W50 (top); Stephen Hutchings, p. W3; Suzanne Mogensen, pp. W23, W39; Andy Myer, pp. 41, W12; Tom Newsom, pp. 25, 49; Dusan Petričic, pp. 17, 18, 24, 42, 43, W7, W15; Gail Piazza, p. 16; Realia/Kirchoff/Wohlberg, Inc., pp. 22, 26, 45, 46; Robert Saunders, p. 37; Steve Schulman, p. W52; Anna Veltfort, p. 35.

ISBNs: 0-13-110635-X (Student's Book with Workbook and Audio CD)
0-13-175039-9 (Student's Book with Workbook and Take-Home Super CD-ROM)

Printed in the United States of America
6 7 8 9 10–QWD–10 09 08

Contents

GRAMMAR BOOSTER

WORKBOOK

Dope = เจ๋ง อ fantastic

Scope and Sequence for 3A and 3B

UNIT	Vocabulary*	Conversation Strategies	Grammar	
1 **Cultural Literacy** *Page 2* *Top Notch* Song: "It's a Great Day for Love"	• Terms for describing manners, etiquette, and culture	• Use <u>By the way</u> to introduce or change a topic • Use expressions such as <u>Do you mind if</u> and <u>Would it be rude to</u> to avoid offending some • Use <u>Actually</u> to politely correct someone • Begin a statement with <u>You know,...</u> to casually shift the focus of a conversation	• Tag questions: form and social use • The past perfect: form and use	• Tag questions: more practice • Verb tense review: simple present, present continuous, present perfect and present perfect continuous, simple past and past continuous, <u>used to</u>, past perfect
2 **Health Matters** *Page 14*	• Dental emergencies • Symptoms • Medical procedures • Types of treatments and practitioners • Medications	• Begin answers with <u>Well</u> to announce a willingness to act • Say <u>That's right</u> to confirm • Use <u>Really?</u> to indicate interest	• <u>May</u>, <u>might</u>, <u>must</u>, and <u>be able to</u>: possibility, conclusions, ability	• <u>May</u>, <u>might</u>, and <u>must</u>: degrees of certainty
3 **Getting Things Done** *Page 26* *Top Notch* Song: "I'll Get Back to You"	• Business and non-business services • Adjectives to describe services • Social events • Steps for planning a social event	• Repeat part of a question to clarify before answering • Begin a sentence with <u>I'm sorry but</u> to politely insist • Use <u>Sure</u> to affirm confidently	• The passive causative • Causatives <u>get</u>, <u>have</u>, and <u>make</u>	• The passive causative: the <u>by</u> phrase • Causatives <u>get</u>, <u>have</u>, and <u>make</u>: more practice • <u>Let</u> followed by an object and base form • Causative <u>have</u> and past perfect auxiliary <u>have</u>
4 **Life Choices** *Page 38*	• Fields for work or study • Reasons for changing your mind • Skills and abilities	• Say <u>Not bad</u> to respond casually to a question about well-being • Use <u>No kidding</u> to convey pleasant surprise • Say <u>Could be</u> to imply that you don't completely agree	• Future in the past: <u>was</u> / <u>were going to</u> and <u>would</u> • Perfect modals: meaning and form	• Review: future with <u>will</u> and <u>be going to</u> • Review: future meaning with present continuous, simple present, and modals • Regrets about the past: <u>wish</u> + the past perfect; <u>should have</u> and <u>ought to have</u>
5 **Holidays and Traditions** *Page 50* *Top Notch* Song: "Endless Holiday"	• Types of holidays • Ways to commemorate a holiday • Wedding terminology	• Use the expression <u>Same to you</u> to acknowledge well-wishes • Preface a question with <u>Do you mind if I ask</u> to make it less abrupt	• Adjective clauses with subject relative pronouns • Adjective clauses with object relative pronouns	• Adjective clauses: more practice • Reciprocal pronouns: <u>each other</u> and <u>one another</u> • Reflexive pronouns • <u>By</u> + reflexive pronouns • Adjective clauses: <u>who</u> and <u>whom</u> for formal English

*In *Top Notch*, the term *vocabulary* refers to individual words, phrases, and expressions.

Speaking	Pronunciation	Listening	Reading	Writing
• Make small talk with a stranger • Ask how someone prefers to be addressed • Get to know someone • Describe rules of etiquette • Discuss cultural changes	• Rising and falling intonation for tag questions	• Radio call-in show on etiquette Task: identify the topics discussed • People introducing themselves Task: determine how people prefer to be addressed	• Flyer for an international language school • Newspaper article about recent changes in Japanese culture • Survey about cultural changes	• Advise visitors about culture and etiquette in your country • Express your opinion on the importance of etiquette
• Make an appointment • Describe dental problems and medical symptoms • Show concern and empathy • Explain preferences in medical treatments • Talk about medications	• Intonation of lists	• Descriptions of dental emergencies Task: identify problems • Describing symptoms Task: check the symptoms described • Conversations between doctors and patients Task: complete patient information forms	• Health advice for international travelers • Overview of conventional and nontraditional health treatments	• Create a checklist for an international trip • Write about the kinds of health care you use • Complete patient information form
• Request express service • Ask for and recommend a service provider • Describe quality of service • Plan a social event	• Emphatic stress to express enthusiasm	• Recommendations for service providers Task: identify the service required • Planning a social event Task: order the steps and note who will do each step • Requesting express service Task: describe customer needs	• Service provider's website • Tourist guide entry on buying custom-made clothing in Hong Kong	• Create an ad for a local service provider • Identify hard-to-find services • Write a story of a man's day, based on a complex illustration
• Greet someone you haven't seen for a while • Explain a change in life and work choices • Express regrets about life decisions • Discuss skills, abilities, and qualifications	• Reduction of have in perfect modals	• Conversations about changes in life plans Task: listen for the reasons the people changed their minds • Interviews at a job fair Task: match interviewees and qualifications • Conversations about regrets Task: infer whether there were regrets	• Work preference inventory • Skills inventory • Magazine article on the lifework of Mahatma Gandhi and Albert Schweitzer	• Recount the work and life decisions you have made and explain any regrets • Report on the life of a great humanitarian
• Ask about and describe holiday traditions • Ask for and give advice about customs • Describe holidays, celebrations, and wedding traditions	• Rhythm: "thought groups"	• Descriptions of holidays Task: identify the type of holiday and celebration • Lecture on traditional Indian wedding customs Task: correct the false statements • Conversations about weddings Task: determine each topic	• Magazine article describing three holiday traditions from around the world	• Describe in detail a holiday tradition in your country

UNIT	Vocabulary	Conversation Strategies	Grammar	
6 **Disasters and Emergencies** *Page 62* *Top Notch* Song: "Lucky to Be Alive"	• News sources • Severe weather events and other disasters • Emergency preparations and supplies • Terminology for discussing disasters	• Say <u>Will do</u> to accede to a request • Use <u>What a shame</u> to demonstrate empathy • Use <u>It says...</u> to indicate that information comes from a known source • Use <u>Thank goodness</u> to express relief	• Indirect speech: imperatives • Indirect speech: <u>say</u> and <u>tell</u>; tense changes	• Punctuation rules for direct speech • Indirect speech: optional tense changes
7 **Books and Magazines** *Page 74*	• Types of books • Ways to describe reading material • Some ways to enjoy reading	• Preface a request with <u>Do you mind if</u> to be more polite • Use <u>Not at all</u> to indicate that one doesn't mind • Say <u>What (adjective + noun)!</u> to express a compliment	• Noun clauses: embedded questions • Noun clauses as direct objects	• Embedded questions: usage and punctuation • Embedded questions with infinitives • Noun clauses with <u>that</u>: after mental activity verbs • Noun clauses with <u>that</u>: after other expressions
8 **Inventions and Technology** *Page 86* *Top Notch* Song: "Reinvent the Wheel"	• Mechanical inventions in history • Ways to describe innovative products	• Use <u>That depends</u> to indicate one needs more information • Say <u>It can happen to anyone</u> to show empathy when responding to an apology	• Conditional sentences: review • The past unreal conditional	• <u>Unless</u> in conditional sentences • Clauses after <u>wish</u> • The unreal conditional: variety of forms
9 **Controversial Issues** *Page 98*	• Political terms and types of governments • Political and social beliefs • Controversial issues • Ways to disagree politely	• Use the expression <u>That's a good question</u> to imply that you are not sure of the answer or you want to avoid answering • Say <u>We'll have to agree to disagree</u> to politely end a disagreement with no hard feelings	• Non-count nouns for abstract ideas • Verbs followed by objects and infinitives	• Count and non-count nouns • Gerunds and infinitives: form • Review: gerunds and infinitives after certain verbs
10 **Enjoying the World** *Page 110*	• Geographical features • Ways to describe possible risks • Dangerous animals and insects • Positive and negative descriptions • Ways to describe the natural world	• Provide a reason to support and strengthen a warning • Use <u>Be sure to</u> to make an enthusiastic suggestion	• Infinitives with <u>too</u> + adjective • Prepositions of place to describe locations	• Infinitives with <u>too</u> + adjective: more practice • Infinitives with <u>enough</u> • Prepositions usage • Proper nouns: capitalization • Proper nouns: use of <u>the</u>

Speaking	Pronunciation	Listening	Reading	Writing
• Convey a message for a third person • Offer an excuse • Report what you heard on the news • Respond to good and bad news • Discuss plans for an emergency • Describe natural disasters	• Direct and indirect speech: rhythm	• Weather reports Task: identify the weather event • Emergency radio broadcast Task: correct incorrect statements and report facts, using indirect speech • News report on natural disasters Task: identify the types of disasters	• Historic news headlines • Magazine article describing variables that affect an earthquake's severity	• Write about a historic disaster • Provide instructions on preparing for a disaster • Explain the factors that contribute to the severity of an earthquake
• Recommend a book • Give and accept a compliment • Explain where you learned something • Evaluate types of reading materials • Describe your reading habits	• Sentence stress in short answers with <u>think</u>, <u>hope</u>, <u>guess</u>, or <u>believe</u>	• Descriptions of reading habits Task: choose each speaker's preferences • Conversations about books Task: identify the type of book and infer if the speaker likes it	• Online bookstore website • Magazine article about the popularity of, and attitudes about, comic books	• Write about your reading habits • Review a book or other material you've read
• Discuss whether to purchase a product • Accept responsibility for a mistake • Reassure someone • Describe a new invention • Compare important inventions	• Contractions with '<u>d</u> (would)	• People describing problems Task: select a useful invention for each person • Discussions of new products Task: determine which adjective best describes each product	• Magazine article describing the importance of the invention of the printing press	• Write about an invention that you think had a great impact
• Ask for and give advice about acceptable conversation topics • State your opinion • Express agreement or disagree politely • Suggest solutions to global problems • Debate pros and cons	• Stress to emphasize meaning	• Conversations about politics and social beliefs Task: determine each person's political orientation • Opinions about controversial ideas Task: infer the speaker's opinion • People arguing their views Task: summarize arguments • Radio news program Task: identify the problems	• Authentic dictionary entries • Magazine article defining global problems	• Describe a local or world problem and offer possible solutions • Write the pros and cons of a controversial issue
• Warn about risks or dangers • Ask and explain where a place is located • Describe a natural setting • Recommend a place for its beauty • Debate a plan for economic development	• Voiced and voiceless <u>th</u>	• People discussing risks Task: infer if the place is safe • Description of a trip Task: identify natural features • Conversations about tourist destinations Task: infer if the speaker recommends going	• Authentic maps • Magazine article describing the pros and cons of eco-tourism	• Describe a spectacular natural setting • Plan an eco-friendly development • Create a tourism advertisement

Acknowledgments

Top Notch International Advisory Board

The authors gratefully acknowledge the substantive and formative contributions of the members of the International Advisory Board.

CHERYL BELL, Middlesex County College, Middlesex, New Jersey, USA • **ELMA CABAHUG**, City College of San Francisco, San Francisco, California, USA • **JO CARAGATA**, Mukogawa Women's University, Hyogo, Japan • **ANN CARTIER**, Palo Alto Adult School, Palo Alto, California, USA • **TERRENCE FELLNER**, Himeji Dokkyo University, Hyogo, Japan • **JOHN FUJIMORI**, Meiji Gakuin High School, Tokyo, Japan • **ARETA ULHANA GALAT**, Escola Superior de Estudos Empresariais e Informática, Curitiba, Brazil • **DOREEN M. GAYLORD**, Kanazawa Technical College, Ishikawa, Japan • **EMILY GEHRMAN**, Newton International College, Garden Grove, California, USA • **ANN-MARIE HADZIMA**, National Taiwan University, Taipei, Taiwan • **KAREN KYONG-AI PARK**, Seoul National University, Seoul, Korea • **ANA PATRICIA MARTÍNEZ VITE DIP. R.S.A.**, Universidad del Valle de México, Mexico City, Mexico • **MICHELLE ANN MERRITT,** Proulex/ Universidad de Guadalajara, Guadalajara, Mexico • **ADRIANNE P. OCHOA**, Georgia State University, Atlanta, Georgia, USA • **LOUIS PARDILLO**, Korea Herald English Institute, Seoul, Korea • **THELMA PERES**, Casa Thomas Jefferson, Brasilia, Brazil • **DIANNE RUGGIERO**, Broward Community College, Davie, Florida, USA • **KEN SCHMIDT**, Tohoku Fukushi University, Sendai, Japan • **ALISA A. TAKEUCHI**, Garden Grove Adult Education, Garden Grove, California, USA • **JOSEPHINE TAYLOR**, Centro Colombo Americano, Bogotá, Colombia • **PATRICIA VECIÑO**, Instituto Cultural Argentino Norteamericano, Buenos Aires, Argentina • **FRANCES WESTBROOK**, AUA Language Center, Bangkok, Thailand

Reviewers and Piloters

Many thanks also to the reviewers and piloters all over the world who reviewed *Top Notch* in its final form.

G. Julian Abaqueta, Huachiew Chalermprakiet University, Samutprakarn, Thailand • **David Aline**, Kanagawa University, Kanagawa, Japan • **Marcia Alves**, Centro Cultural Brasil Estados Unidos, Franca, Brazil • **Yousef Al-Yacoub**, Qatar Petroleum, Doha, Qatar • **Maristela Barbosa Silveira e Silva**, Instituto Cultural Brasil-Estados Unidos, Manaus, Brazil • **Beth Bartlett**, Centro Colombo Americano, Cali, Colombia • **Carla Battigelli**, University of Zulia, Maracaibo, Venezuela • **Claudia Bautista**, C.B.C., Caracas, Venezuela • **Rob Bell**, Shumei Yachiyo High School, Chiba, Japan • **Dr. Maher Ben Moussa**, Sharjah University, Sharjah, United Arab Emirates • **Elaine Cantor**, Englewood Senior High School, Jacksonville, Florida, USA • **María Aparecida Capellari**, SENAC, São Paulo, Brazil • **Eunice Carrillo Ramos**, Colegio Durango, Naucalpan, Mexico • **Janette Carvalhinho de Oliveira**, Centro de Linguas (UFES), Vitória, Brazil • **María Amelia Carvalho Fonseca**, Centro Cultural Brasil-Estados Unidos, Belém, Brazil • **Audy Castañeda**, Instituto Pedagógico de Caracas, Caracas, Venezuela • **Ching-Fen Chang**, National Chiao Tung University, Hsinchu, Taiwan • **Ying-Yu Chen**, Chinese Culture University, Taipei, Taiwan • **Joyce Chin**, The Language Training and Testing Center, Taipei, Taiwan • **Eun Cho**, Pagoda Language School, Seoul, Korea • **Hyungzung Cho**, MBC Language Institute, Seoul, Korea • **Dong Sua Choi**, MBC Language Institute, Seoul, Korea • **Jeong Mi Choi**, Freelancer, Seoul, Korea • **Peter Chun**, Pagoda Language School, Seoul, Korea • **Eduardo Corbo**, Legacy ELT, Salto, Uruguay • **Marie Cosgrove**, Surugadai University, Saitama, Japan • **María Antonieta Covarrubias Souza**, Centro Escolar Akela, Mexico City, Mexico • **Katy Cox**, Casa Thomas Jefferson, Brasilia, Brazil • **Michael Donovan**, Gakushuin University, Tokyo, Japan • **Stewart Dorward**, Shumei Eiko High School, Saitama, Japan • **Ney Eric Espina**, Centro Venezolano Americano del Zulia, Maracaibo, Venezuela • **Edith Espino**, Centro Especializado de Lenguas - Universidad Tecnológica de Panamá, El Dorado, Panama • **Allen P. Fermon**, Instituto Brasil-Estados Unidos, Ceará, Brazil • **Simão Ferreira Banha**, Phil Young's English School, Curitiba, Brazil • **María Elena Flores Lara**, Colegio Mercedes, Mexico City, Mexico • **Valesca Fróis Nassif**, Associação Cultural Brasil-Estados Unidos, Salvador, Brazil • **José Fuentes**, Empire Language Consulting, Caracas, Venezuela • **José Luis Guerrero**, Colegio Cristobal Colón, Mexico City, Mexico • **Claudia Patricia Gutiérrez**, Centro Colombo Americano, Cali, Colombia • **Valerie Hansford**, Asia University, Tokyo, Japan • **Gene Hardstark**, Dotkyo University, Saitama, Japan • **Maiko Hata**, Kansai University, Osaka, Japan • **Susan Elizabeth Haydock Miranda de Araujo**, Centro Cultural Brasil Estados Unidos, Belém, Brazil • **Gabriela Herrera**, Fundametal, Valencia, Venezuela • **Sandy Ho**, GEOS International, New York, New York, USA • **Yuri Hosoda**, Showa Women's University, Tokyo, Japan • **Hsiao-I Hou**, Shu-Te University, Kaohsiung County, Taiwan • **Kuei-ping Hsu**, National Tsing Hua University, Hsinchu, Taiwan • **Chia-yu Huang**, National Tsing Hua University, Hsinchu, Taiwan • **Caroline C. Hwang**, National Taipei University of Science and Technology, Taipei, Taiwan • **Diana Jones**, Angloamericano, Mexico City, Mexico • **Eunjeong Kim**, Freelancer, Seoul, Korea • **Julian Charles King**, Qatar Petroleum, Doha, Qatar • **Bruce Lee**, CIE: Foreign Language Institute, Seoul, Korea • **Myunghee Lee**, MBC Language Institute, Seoul, Korea • **Naidnapa Leoprasertkul**, Language Development Center, Mahasarakham University, Mahasarakham, Thailand • **Eleanor S. Leu**, Souchow University, Taipei, Taiwan • **Eliza Liu**, Chinese Culture University, Taipei, Taiwan • **Carlos Lizárraga**, Angloamericano, Mexico City, Mexico • **Philippe Loussarevian**, Keio University Shonan Fujisawa High School, Kanagawa, Japan • **Jonathan Lynch**, Azabu University, Tokyo, Japan • **Thomas Mach**, Konan University, Hyogo, Japan • **Lilian Mandel Civatti**, Associação Cultural Brasil-Estados Unidos, Salvador, Brazil • **Hakan Mansuroglu**, Zoni Language Center, West New York, New Jersey, USA • **Martha McGaughey**, Language Training Institute, Englewood Cliffs, New Jersey, USA • **David Mendoza Plascencia**, Instituto Internacional de Idiomas, Naucalpan, Mexico • **Theresa Mezo**, Interamerican University, Río Piedras, Puerto Rico • **Luz Adriana Montenegro Silva**, Colegio CAFAM, Bogotá, Colombia • **Magali de Moraes Menti**, Instituto Lingua, Porto Alegre, Brazil • **Massoud Moslehpour**, The Overseas Chinese Institute of Technology, Taichung, Taiwan • **Jennifer Nam**, IKE, Seoul, Korea • **Marcos Norelle F. Victor**, Instituto Brasil-Estados Unidos, Ceará, Brazil • **Luz María Olvera**, Instituto Juventud del Estado de México, Naucalpan, Mexico • **Roxana Orrego Ramírez**, Universidad Diego Portales, Santiago, Chile • **Ming-Jong Pan**, National Central University, Jhongli City, Taiwan • **Sandy Park**, Topia Language School, Seoul, Korea • **Patrícia Elizabeth Peres Martins**, Instituto Brasil-Estados Unidos, Rio de Janeiro, Brazil • **Rodrigo Peza**, Passport Language Centers, Bogotá, Colombia • **William Porter**, Osaka Institute of Technology, Osaka, Japan • **Caleb Prichard**, Kwansei Gakuin University, Hyogo, Japan • **Mirna Quintero**, Instituto Pedagógico de Caracas, Caracas, Venezuela • **Roberto Rabbini**, Seigakuin University, Saitama, Japan • **Terri Rapoport**, Berkeley College, White Plains, New York, USA • **Yvette Rieser**, Centro Electrónico de Idiomas, Maracaibo, Venezuela • **Orlando Rodríguez**, New English Teaching School, Paysandu, Uruguay • **Mayra Rosario**, Pontificia Universidad Católica Madre y Maestra, Santiago, Dominican Republic • **Peter Scout**, Sakura no Seibo Junior College, Fukushima, Japan • **Jungyeon Shim**, EG School, Seoul, Korea • **Keum Ok Song**, MBC Language Institute, Seoul, Korea • **Assistant Professor Dr. Reongrudee Soonthornmanee**, Chulalongkorn University Language Institute, Bangkok, Thailand • **Claudia Stanisclause**, The Language College, Maracay, Venezuela • **Tom Suh**, The Princeton Review, Seoul, Korea • **Phiphawin Suphawat**, KhonKaen University, KhonKaen, Thailand • **Craig Sweet**, Poole Gakuin Junior and Senior High Schools, Osaka, Japan • **Yi-nien Josephine Twu**, National Tsing Hua University, Hsinchu, Taiwan • **Maria Christina Uchôa Close**, Instituto Cultural Brasil-Estados Unidos, São José dos Campos, Brazil • **Luz Vanegas Lopera**, Lexicom The Place For Learning English, Medellín, Colombia • **Julieta Vasconcelos García**, Centro Escolar del Lago, A.C., Mexico City, Mexico • **Carol Vaughan**, Kanto Kokusai High School, Tokyo, Japan • **Patricia Celia Veciño**, Instituto Cultural Argentino Norteamericano, Buenos Aires, Argentina • **Isabela Villas Boas**, Casa Thomas Jefferson, Brasilia, Brazil • **Iole Vitti**, Peanuts English School, Poços de Caldas, Brazil • **Gabi Witthaus**, Qatar Petroleum, Doha, Qatar • **Yi-Ling Wu**, Shih Chien University, Taipei, Taiwan • **Chad Wynne**, Osaka Keizai University, Osaka, Japan • **Belkis Yanes**, Freelance Instructor, Caracas, Venezuela • **I-Chieh Yang**, Chung-kuo Institute of Technology, Taipei, Taiwan • **Emil Ysona**, Instituto Cultural Dominico-Americano, Santo Domingo, Dominican Republic • **Chi-fang Yu**, Soo Chow University, Taipei, Taiwan • **Shigeki Yusa**, Sendai Shirayuri Women's College, Sendai, Japan

To the Teacher

What is *Top Notch*?

- *Top Notch* is a six-level communicative English course for adults and young adults, with two beginning entry levels.
- *Top Notch* prepares students to interact successfully and confidently with both native and non-native speakers of English.
- *Top Notch* demonstrably brings students to a "Top Notch" level of communicative competence.

Key Elements of the *Top Notch* Instructional Design

Concise two-page lessons

Each easy-to-teach two-page lesson is designed for one class session and begins with a clearly stated communication goal and ends with controlled or free communication practice. Each lesson provides vocabulary, grammar, and social language contextualized in all four skills, keeping the pace of a class session lively and varied.

Daily confirmation of progress

Adult and young adult students need to observe and confirm their own progress. In *Top Notch*, students conclude each class session with a controlled or free practice activity that demonstrates their ability to use new vocabulary, grammar, and social language. This motivates and keeps students eager to continue their study of English and builds their pride in being able to speak accurately, fluently, and authentically.

Real language

Carefully exposing students to authentic, natural English, both receptively and productively, is a necessary component of building understanding and expression. All conversation models feature the language people really use; nowhere to be found is "textbook English" written merely to exemplify grammar.

Practical content

In addition to classic topical vocabulary, grammar, and conversation, *Top Notch* includes systematic practice of highly practical language, such as: how to describe symptoms at a doctor's office, and how to ask for express service at a service provider such as a dry cleaner or copy center. In addition

to these practical applications, *Top Notch* continues development of its discussion syllabus with popular discussion topics ranging from explaining the holiday customs of one's country to polite discussions of government and politics—usable language today's students want and need.

Memorable model conversations

Effective language instruction must make language memorable. The full range of social and functional communicative needs is presented through practical model conversations that are intensively practiced and manipulated, first within a guided model and then in freer and more personalized formats.

High-impact vocabulary syllabus

In order to ensure students' solid acquisition of vocabulary essential for communication, *Top Notch* contains explicit presentation, practice, and systematic extended recycling of words, collocations, and expressions appropriate at each level of study. The extensive captioned illustrations, photos, definitions, examples, and contextualized sentences remove doubts about meaning and provide a permanent in-book reference for student test preparation. An added benefit is that teachers don't have to search for pictures to bring to class and don't have to resort to translating vocabulary into the students' native language.

Learner-supportive grammar

Grammar is approached explicitly and cognitively, through form, meaning, and use—both within the Student's Book units and in a bound-in Grammar Booster. Charts provide examples and paradigms enhanced by simple usage notes at students' level of comprehension. This takes the guesswork out of meaning, makes lesson preparation easier for teachers, and provides students with comprehensible charts for permanent reference and test preparation. All presentations of grammar are followed by exercises to ensure adequate practice.

English as an international language

Top Notch prepares students for interaction with both native and non-native speakers of English, both linguistically and culturally. English is treated as an international language, rather than the language of a particular country or region. In addition, *Top Notch* helps students develop a cultural fluency by creating an awareness of the varied rules across cultures for: politeness, greetings and introductions, appropriateness of dress in different settings, conversation do's and taboos, table manners, and other similar issues.

Two beginning-level texts

Beginning students can be placed either in *Top Notch 1* or *Top Notch Fundamentals*, depending on ability and background. Even absolute beginners can start with confidence in *Top Notch Fundamentals*. False beginners can begin with *Top Notch 1*. The *Top Notch Placement Test* clarifies the best placement within the series.

Estimated teaching time

Each level of *Top Notch* is designed for 60 to 90 instructional hours and contains a full range of supplementary components and enrichment devices to tailor the course to individual needs.

Components of *Top Notch 3*

Student's Book with Take-Home Super CD-ROM

The Super CD-ROM includes a variety of exciting interactive activities: Speaking Practice, Interactive Workbook, Games and Puzzles, and *Top Notch Pop* Karaoke. The disk can also be played on an audio CD player to listen to the Conversation Models and the *Top Notch Pop* songs.

Teacher's Edition and Lesson Planner

Complete yet concise lesson plans are provided for each class. Corpus notes provide essential information from the *Longman Spoken American Corpus* and the *Longman Learner's Corpus*. In addition, a free *Teacher's Resource Disk* offers the following printable extension activities to personalize your teaching style:

- Grammar self-checks
- *Top Notch Pop* song activities
- Writing process worksheets
- Learning strategies
- Pronunciation activities and supplements
- Extra reading comprehension activities
- Vocabulary cards and cumulative vocabulary activities
- Graphic organizers
- Pair work cards

Copy & Go: Ready-made Interactive Activities for Busy Teachers

Interactive games, puzzles, and other practice activities in convenient photocopiable form support the Student's Book content and provide a welcome change of pace.

Complete Classroom Audio Program

The audio program contains listening comprehension activities, rhythm and intonation practice, and targeted pronunciation activities that focus on accurate and comprehensible pronunciation.

Because *Top Notch* prepares students for international communication, a variety of native *and* non-native speakers are included to ready students for the world outside the classroom. The audio program also includes the five *Top Notch Pop* songs in standard and karaoke form.

Workbook

A tightly linked illustrated Workbook contains exercises that provide additional practice and reinforcement of language concepts and skills from *Top Notch* and its Grammar Booster.

Complete Assessment Package with *ExamView®* Software

Ten easy-to-administer and easy-to-score unit achievement tests assess listening, vocabulary, grammar, social language, reading, and writing. Two review tests, one mid-book and one end-of-book, provide additional cumulative assessment. Two speaking tests assess progress in speaking. In addition to the photocopiable achievement tests, *ExamView®* software enables teachers to tailor-make tests to best meet their needs by combining items in any way they wish.

Top Notch TV

A lively and entertaining video offers a TV-style situation comedy that reintroduces language from each *Top Notch* unit, plus authentic unrehearsed interviews with English speakers from around the world and authentic karaoke. Packaged with the video are activity worksheets and a booklet with teaching suggestions and complete video scripts.

Companion Website

A Companion Website at www.longman.com/topnotch provides numerous additional resources for students and teachers. This no-cost, high-benefit feature includes opportunities for further practice of language and content from the *Top Notch* Student's Book.

Welcome to Top Notch!

About the Authors

Joan Saslow

Joan Saslow has taught English as a Foreign Language and English as a Second Language to adults and young adults in both South America and the United States. She taught English and French at the Binational Centers of Valparaíso and Viña del Mar, Chile, and the Catholic University of Valparaíso. In the United States, Ms. Saslow taught English as a Foreign Language to Japanese university students at Marymount College and to international students in Westchester Community College's intensive English program as well as workplace English at the General Motors auto assembly plant in Tarrytown, NY.

Ms. Saslow is the series director of Longman's popular five-level adult series *True Colors: An EFL Course for Real Communication* and of *True Voices*, a five-level video course. She is author of *Ready to Go: Language, Lifeskills, and Civics*, a four-level adult ESL series; *Workplace Plus*, a vocational English series; and of *Literacy Plus*, a two-level series that teaches literacy, English, and culture to adult pre-literate students. She is also author of *English in Context: Reading Comprehension for Science and Technology*, a three-level series for English for special purposes. In addition, Ms. Saslow has been an author, an editor of language teaching materials, a teacher-trainer, and a frequent speaker at gatherings of EFL and ESL teachers for over thirty years.

Allen Ascher

Allen Ascher has been a teacher and teacher-trainer in both China and the United States, as well as an administrator and a publisher. Mr. Ascher specialized in teaching listening and speaking to students at the Beijing Second Foreign Language Institute, to hotel workers at a major international hotel in China, and to Japanese students from Chubu University studying English at Ohio University. In New York, Mr. Ascher taught students of all language backgrounds and abilities at the City University of New York, and he trained teachers in the TESOL Certificate Program at the New School. He was also the academic director of the International English Language Institute at Hunter College.

Mr. Ascher has provided lively workshops for EFL teachers throughout Asia, Latin America, Europe, and the Middle East. He is author of the popular *Think about Editing: A Grammar Editing Guide for ESL Writers*. As a publisher, Mr. Ascher played a key role in the creation of some of the most widely used materials for adults, including: *True Colors, NorthStar, Focus on Grammar, Global Links*, and *Ready to Go*. Mr. Ascher has an M.A. in Applied Linguistics from Ohio University.

Cultural Literacy

UNIT GOALS

1 Meet someone and make small talk
2 Get to know someone
3 Be culturally literate
4 Discuss how culture changes over time

A **TOPIC PREVIEW.** Look at the flyer for an international language school. Choose a place to study English.

Study Abroad Opportunities

EnglishSOURCE
YOUR TICKET TO THE WORLD OF ENGLISH

Choose from one of our 9 international sites

Sydney

Harbor city with a cultural flair

Auckland

With a background rhythm of Polynesian culture

Cape Town

Pristine beaches and a cultural melting pot

Shop and compare. EnglishSOURCE offers:

- an international student body—over 35 countries represented!
- courses tailored to your available time—from one week to one year

- native teachers with university degrees
- arranged homestays near classes
- guaranteed achievement—or your money back!

Cambridge

Historic city—world-renowned university—community of scholars

Edinburgh

Magnificent—from the medieval to the modern

New York

Capital of the world

London

The birthplace of English—home of the Crown

San Francisco

Human-size city—a delight for the eyes—near ocean and mountain peaks

Toronto

Canada's largest city—never run out of things to do, see, or buy

B **PAIR WORK.** Which site did you choose? Why?

☐ because of the location
☐ because of the type of English spoken there

☐ because I have friends or relatives there
☐ other reason(s): _____

C 🎧 **SOUND BITES.** **Read along silently as you listen to a conversation at a business meeting in Thailand.**

TERESA: Allow me to introduce myself. I'm Teresa Segovia, from Santiago, Chile. *Sawatdee-Kaa.*
SURAT: Where did you learn the *wai*?*
TERESA: Actually, a Thai friend in Chile taught me.

*Thais greet each other with a gesture called the "wai" and by saying "Sawatdee-Kaa" (women) / "Sawatdee-Khrab (men)."

SURAT: *Sawatdee-Khrab.* Nice to meet you, Ms. Segovia. I'm Surat Leekpai.
TERESA: Nice to meet you, too. But please call me Terri.
SURAT: And please call me Surat. It's easier to say than Leekpai!

TERESA: Do you mind my asking you the custom here? Are most people on a first-name basis?
SURAT: At company meetings in English, absolutely. In general, though, it's probably best to watch what others do. You know what they say: "When in Rome…"
TERESA: M-hmm… "do as the Romans do!"

D **DISCUSSION.**

1. Why do you think Teresa greets Surat with the *wai*?

2. Why do Surat and Teresa say, "When in Rome, do as the Romans do!"?

3. When do you think people should use first names with each other? When do you think they should use titles and last names?

WHAT ABOUT **YOU?**

If you take a trip to another country, how would you like to be addressed?

☐ **1.** I'd like to be called by my title and my family name.
☐ **2.** I'd like to be called by my first name.
☐ **3.** I'd like to be called by my nickname.
☐ **4.** I'd prefer to follow the local customs.

Meet Someone and Make Small Talk

light talk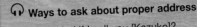

⌂ CONVERSATION
MODEL Read and listen.

A: Good morning. Beautiful day, isn't it?

B: It really is. By the way, I'm Kazuko Toshinaga.

A: I'm Jane Quitt. Nice to meet you.

B: Nice to meet you, too.

A: Do you mind if I call you Kazuko?

B: Absolutely not. Please do.

A: And please call me Jane.

⌂ **Rhythm and intonation practice**

Do you mind if ...?
*   - No, I don't (It's ok)*
*   - Yes, I do.*

> ⌂ **Ways to ask about proper address**
>
> Do you mind if I call you [Kazuko]?
> Would it be rude to call you [Kazuko]?
> What would you like to be called?
> How do you prefer to be addressed?
> Do you use Ms. or Mrs.?

WILDLIF
CENTE
NATUR
TOUR

A ▸ GRAMMAR. Tag questions: form and social use

Use tag questions to confirm information you already think is true or to encourage someone to make small talk. *PS. use only pronouns. , use V. to/u Tag   she has four kids, doesn't she?*   *she has never visited CA, has she*

statement	tag question	answer
You're Kazuko,	**aren't you?**	Yes, I am. / No, I'm not.
You speak Thai,	**don't you?**	Yes, I do. / No, I don't.
They'll be here later,	**won't they?**	Yes, they will. / No, they won't.
They didn't know,	**did they?**	Yes, they did. / No, they didn't.
It's a beautiful day,	**isn't it?**	Yes, it is. / No, it isn't.

When the statement is affirmative, the tag question is negative. When the statement is negative, the tag question is affirmative.

He's late, **isn't** he?   He **isn't** late, **is** he?

BE CAREFUL! Use pronouns, not names or nouns, in tag questions.

Machu Picchu was built by the Incas, **wasn't it?** (NOT ~~wasn't Machu Picchu?~~)

Use aren't for negative tag questions after I am.

I'm on time, **aren't** I? BUT I'm not late, am I?

auxilliry/helping v.   main v.

They will go on vacation, won't they?

GRAMMAR BOOSTER

PAGE G1
For more ...

B ▸ ⌂ PRONUNCIATION. Intonation of tag questions. Read and listen.
Then listen again and repeat.

Use rising intonation when you're not sure if the listener will agree, and you expect an answer.

People use first names here, don't they?

That movie was great, wasn't it?

Use falling intonation when you think the listener will agree.

(sure)

It's a beautiful day for a walk, isn't it?

You're studying in Chicago next year, aren't you?

C **Complete each statement with a tag question.**

1. Robert Reston is the director of the English program, _isn't he_ ?

2. There weren't any openings at the San Francisco location, _were there_ ?

3. They're all going to enroll in the Chicago course, _aren't they_ ?

4. I'm not too late to sign up, _am I_ ?

5. She prefers to be addressed by her title and last name, _doesn't she_ ?

6. The letters of acceptance will be mailed in March, _won't they_ ?

7. Australia has been a terrific place to learn English, _hasn't it_ ? ถ้ามี V. 2 ตัว ใช้ได้ V.ตัวแรกใน ประโยค Tag question

8. It was a great day, _wasn't it_ ?

D **PAIR WORK. Write a few facts about yourself. Give the paper to your partner to read for a minute. Then take back the paper and confirm the information with tag questions.**

> " Your parents are from Italy, aren't they? "

I grew up here, but my parents are from Italy. I started studying English when I was in primary school.

CONVERSATION
PAIR WORK

Meet your classmates. Ask them how they'd like to be addressed. Use tag questions to make small talk about the weather and other subjects.

CONTROLLED PRACTICE

Get to Know Someone

🎧 CONVERSATION
MODEL Read and listen.

A: Hi. I'm Sylvia Contreras.

B: Conrad Schmitt. Nice to meet you, Sylvia. You know, you look familiar. You were in this class last term, weren't you?

A: No, actually, I wasn't. I hadn't arrived here yet when the class began.

🎧 **Rhythm and intonation practice**

had + V₃ (past participle)

A **GRAMMAR.** The past perfect: form and use

Form the past perfect with <u>had</u> and a past participle of the main verb.

past participle
By 2001, she **had** already **met** her husband.

Use the past perfect to describe something that happened before a specific time in the past.

By April, he **had started** his new job.
At 3:00, we **hadn't** yet **heard** the news.

Use the past perfect with the simple past tense to show which of two past events occurred first.

I **had** already **seen** the movie when it **came** out on DVD. (First I saw it. Then it came out on DVD.)

Note that in informal speech we often use the simple past tense instead of the past perfect. The words <u>before</u> and <u>after</u> can help clarify the order of the events in informal speech.

By April, he started his new job.
Before I graduated, I learned to speak Greek.
I became a good driver after I got my own car.

PAGES G1–G3
For more …

B **Choose the correct meaning for each statement.**

1. "When they decided to open a language school in Scotland, I had already decided to study in San Francisco."
   - ☐ First they decided to open the language school in Scotland. Then I decided to study in San Francisco.
   - ☑ First I decided to study in San Francisco. Then they opened a language school in Scotland.

2. "By the time she was twenty, she had studied at two language schools."
   - ☐ She turned twenty before she studied at two language schools.
   - ☑ First she studied at two language schools. Then she turned twenty.

3. "We had already applied for the study abroad program when they canceled it."
   - ☑ First we applied for the program. Then they canceled it.
   - ☐ First they canceled the program. Then we applied for it.

4. "I had received my acceptance letter when they closed the school."
   ☒ First I received my acceptance letter. Then they closed the school.
   ☐ First they closed the school. Then I received my acceptance letter.

C **Lynn Todd is taking a weekend trip. It's almost 6:00 P.M. Read her "to-do" list and complete the statements, using <u>already</u> or <u>not yet</u>.**

1. At 8:30 Lynn _had already dropped off_ her jacket, but she _hadn't yet taken_ the cats to Mara's house.

2. By 11:00 she _had already taken_ the cats to Mara's house, but she _hadn't yet packed_ for the weekend.

3. At 12:45 she _hadn't yet had/eaten_ lunch with Lainie, but she _had already picked up_ the car.

4. By 2:10 she _had already returned_ the books to the library, but she _hadn't yet had/taken_ her exam.

5. At 5:15 she _hadn't yet picked up_ Paul, but she _had already picked up_ her jacket at the dry cleaners.

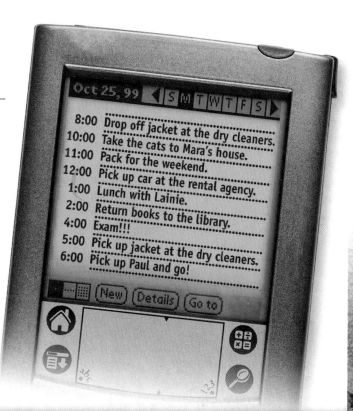

Oct 25, 99 ◀ S M T W T F S ▶

8:00 Drop off jacket at the dry cleaners.
10:00 Take the cats to Mara's house.
11:00 Pack for the weekend.
12:00 Pick up car at the rental agency.
1:00 Lunch with Lainie.
2:00 Return books to the library.
4:00 Exam!!!
5:00 Pick up jacket at the dry cleaners.
6:00 Pick up Paul and go!

[New] [Details] [Go to]

CONVERSATION
PAIR WORK

Role-play getting to know someone, using one of the imaginary situations. Use the guide, or create a new conversation.

A: _____ , I'm _____ .

B: _____ . Nice to meet you, _____ . You know, you look familiar. _____ ?

A: _____ …

Continue the conversation in your <u>own</u> way.

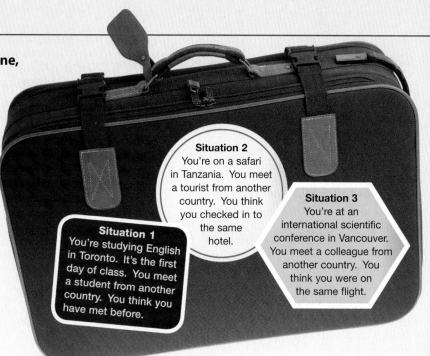

Situation 1
You're studying English in Toronto. It's the first day of class. You meet a student from another country. You think you have met before.

Situation 2
You're on a safari in Tanzania. You meet a tourist from another country. You think you checked in to the same hotel.

Situation 3
You're at an international scientific conference in Vancouver. You meet a colleague from another country. You think you were on the same flight.

CONTROLLED PRACTICE

Be Culturally Literate

A ∩ VOCABULARY. Manners and etiquette. Listen and practice.

(n) **etiquette** the "rules" of polite behavior
อริยเคราะห์

When traveling, it's important to be aware of the etiquette of the culture you will be visiting.

cultural literacy knowing about and respecting the culture of others and following their rules of etiquette when interacting with them
extreamly important

In today's world, cultural literacy is essential to success and good relations with others.

(n) **table manners** rules for polite behavior when eating with other people

Table manners differ from culture to culture.

punctuality the social "rules" about being on time

Punctuality is considered more important in some cultures than in others.

(adj) **impolite** not polite, rude

All cultures have rules for polite and impolite behavior.

(adj) **offensive** extremely rude or impolite

In some cultures, it's offensive to take pictures of people without their permission.

customary usual or traditional in a particular culture

In many cultures, handshakes are customary when meeting someone for the first time.

taboo not allowed because of very strong cultural or religious rules against behavior or topics that are considered very offensive

It's taboo to eat pork in some religions.

B DISCUSSION.

1. What are some good ways to teach children etiquette? Give specific examples, using words from the vocabulary.

2. Do you know any differences between your culture and others?

3. Why do you think table manners are important in almost all cultures?

modest = conservative

C ∩ LISTENING COMPREHENSION. Listen to three calls from a radio show. Then look at the chart and listen again to each call. Check the subjects that were discussed.

What subjects were discussed?	1. Arturo and Jettrin	2. Hiroko and Nadia	3. Javier and Sujeet
table manners	☐	☐	☑
greetings	☑	☐	☐
dress and clothing	☐	☑	☐
male and female behavior	☐	☑	☐
taboos	☑	☐	☑
offensive behavior	☐	☑	☑
punctuality	☐	☐	☐
language	☐	☑	☐

D DISCUSSION. In small groups, summarize the information from each of the calls on the radio show. Listen again if necessary.

INTERACTION • *Know before you go!*

STEP 1. PAIR WORK.
On the notepad, make notes about what visitors to your country should know.

STEP 2. DISCUSSION.
Combine everyone's notes on the board. Does everyone agree?

STEP 3. WRITING.
Write an article to help a visitor be culturally literate about your country. Use important information from your notepad and the board.

How do people greet each other when they meet for the first time?

Are greetings customs different for men and women? How?

When and how do you address people formally?

When and how do you address people informally?

What are some do's and don'ts for table manners?

Are certain foods or beverages taboo?

What are some taboo conversation topics?

What are the customs about punctuality?

What is a customary gift if you are visiting someone's home?

Are there any gift taboos (kinds of flowers, etc.)?

Are there some situations or places where you should dress modestly?

What else should a visitor know?

4 Discuss How Culture Changes over Time

A READING WARM-UP. Can you think of an example of how etiquette and culture change over time?

B ◯ **READING.** Read the article. Is Japanese culture more or less formal than it was in the past?

Japanese Workers Get Word from on High: Drop Formality

By NORIMITSU ONISHI

HIROSHIMA, Japan, Oct. 30, 2003 — The change in policy came directly from the Tokyo headquarters of Elpida Memory, a semiconductor maker.

Elpida's 1,366 workers were told to stop addressing each other by their titles and simply to add the suffix -san to their names. Many Japanese have dropped the use of titles to create a more open — and, they hope, competitive — culture. This change mirrors other changes in Japanese society, experts say. Equality-minded parents no longer emphasize honorific language to their children, and most schools no longer expect children to use honorific language to their teachers. What is clear is that the use of honorific language, called keigo, to elevate a person or humble one-self, has especially fallen out of use among young Japanese.

Naomi Sugi, a secretary at the Elpida factory, has hesitantly begun addressing her boss as "Mr. Yamamoto" instead of "President Yamamoto."

Japanese, perhaps more than any other language, has long taken account of social standing. In Japanese, there are many ways to say I or you, calibrated by age, circumstance, gender, social position and other factors. Verb endings, adjectives and entire words also shift according to the situation.

These days, companies hope the use of -san — less cumbersome than the longer titles traditionally used — will allow workers to exchange ideas more freely and make decisions more quickly. In 2001, 59 percent of companies with more than 3,000 employees had adopted such a policy, compared with 34 percent in 1995, according to the Institute of Labor Administration of Japan.

"It's easier to talk now," said Kazuyoshi Iizuka, a 32-year-old employee at the Tokyo headquarters of Elpida. The factory's president, Takehiko Kubota, 59, who describes himself as "old-fashioned," sent an e-mail message on Sept. 5 explaining the policy to his staff.

SOURCE: The *New York Times*, Oct. 30, 2003 Copyright © 2003 by The New York Times Co. Reprinted with permission.

C Answer the following questions, according to the information in the article.

1. What are some recent changes in the social use of the Japanese language?

2. How has Japanese business culture changed?

D DISCUSSION. What do you think could be some positive and negative results of the changes described in the article?

INTERACTION • *Is change for the better?*

STEP 1. **Have cultural features changed a little or a lot in the last fifty years? Complete the survey.**

Culture Survey

	have changed a little	have changed a lot	Is the change for the better? (YES or NO)	
1. Table manners	☐	☑	☑	☐
2. Musical tastes	☐	☑	☑	☐
3. Dating customs	☐	☑	☑	☐
4. Clothing customs	☐	☑	☑	☐
5. Rules about formal behavior	☐	☑	☑	☐
6. Rules about punctuality	☐	☑	☑	☐
7. Forms of address =call	☐	☑	☑	☐
8. Male / female roles in the workplace	☐	☑	☑	☐
9. Male / female roles in the home	☐	☑	☑	☐

Total YES answers: _____

Are you a dinosaur or a chameleon?

How many times did you check YES in the third column?

0–3 = Definitely a dinosaur.
You prefer to stick with tradition. Your motto: "If it isn't broken, don't fix it!"

4–6 = A little of both. You're willing to adapt to change, but not too fast. Your motto: "Easy does it!"

7–9 = Definitely a chameleon.
You adapt to change easily. Your motto: "Out with the old, in with the new!"

STEP 2. PAIR WORK. Compare and discuss your answers and give specific examples of changes for each answer.

> " I think clothing customs have become less modest. My mother had to wear a uniform to school. But by the time I started school, girls had stopped wearing them. Now girls can go to school in jeans and even shorts! "

STEP 3. DISCUSSION.

- What are the advantages and disadvantages of the changes in your culture? Does everyone think change is good?
- Do older and younger people disagree about culture change? Do men and women disagree?

NEED HELP? **Here's language you already know:**

Formality and informality
be on a first-name basis
prefer to be addressed by their first [last] names / titles and family names

Agree about facts
[People don't use titles as much], do they?
[Clothing customs used to be more modest], didn't they?

Agree in general
I agree. I think you're right.

Disagree in general
I disagree.
Actually, I don't agree, because ——.
Really? I think ——.

A 🎧 **LISTENING COMPREHENSION.** **Listen to the conversations of people introducing themselves. Check the statement in each pair that's true.**

1. ☐ She'd like to be addressed by her title and family name.
   ☐ She'd like to be addressed by her first name.

2. ☐ She'd prefer to be called by her first name.
   ☐ She'd prefer to be called by her title and last name.

3. ☐ It's customary to call people by their first name there.
   ☐ It's not customary to call people by their first name there.

4. ☐ He's comfortable with the policy about names.
   ☐ He's not comfortable with the policy about names.

5. ☐ She prefers to use the title Mrs.
   ☐ She prefers to use the title Dr.

> **TOP NOTCH SONG**
> "It's a Great Day for Love"
> Lyrics on last page before
> Workbook.

> **TOP NOTCH PROJECT**
> Make a cultural literacy
> guidebook. Find cultural
> information about countries
> you'd like to visit on the
> Internet.

> **TOP NOTCH WEBSITE**
> For Unit 1 online activities,
> visit the *Top Notch*
> Companion Website at
> www.longman.com/topnotch.

B **Complete each statement with a tag question.**

1. You're not from around here, _____?

2. You were in this class last year, _____?

3. They haven't been here since yesterday, _____?

4. It's impolite to ask people their age, _____?

5. These chrysanthemums are an OK gift here, _____?

6. I met you on the tour in Nepal, _____?

7. We'll have a chance to discuss this tomorrow, _____?

8. By 10:00 he had already picked up her passport, _____?

C **Complete each statement.**

1. Behaving impolitely when eating with others is an example of bad _____ .

2. Each country has customs and traditions about how to behave in social situations. The rules are sometimes called _____ .

3. Each culture has its own sense of _____ . It's important to understand people's ideas about lateness.

A chrysanthemum.
Chrysanthemums are
an inappropriate social
gift in some countries.

D **WRITING.** **Is etiquette important? On a separate sheet of paper, explain your opinion. Include some or all of the words in the box.**

impolite	polite	taboo
table manners	formal	informal

UNIT WRAP-UP

- **Grammar.** Make statements with question tags about the picture.
  Machu Picchu is really interesting, isn't it?

- **Social Language.** Create conversations for the people on the tour.
  A: Do you mind if I call you Jane?
  B: Absolutely not. Please do.

- **Writing.** Write about the people in the picture.
  There are people from different cultures on the tour ...

✔ **Now I can ...**

☐ meet someone and make small talk.
☐ get to know someone.
☐ be culturally literate.
☐ discuss how culture changes over time.

13

Health Matters

UNIT GOALS

1 Make an appointment to see a dentist
2 Describe symptoms at a doctor's office
3 Discuss types of medical treatments
4 Talk about medications

A ▸ **TOPIC PREVIEW.** Read the health checklist for international travelers. Which tips do you think are the most important?

Before you go...

A checklist for international travelers

✓ **Vaccinations**

You may be required to get vaccinated before you are allowed to enter certain countries. Check the immunization requirements of the country you are visiting. The farther "off the beaten path" you travel, the more important it is to be protected from illness and disease.

✓ **Eyewear**

If you wear glasses or contact lenses, get a copy of your prescription before you go. Carry it with you in case you break or lose your eyewear. Or be sure to carry an extra pair with you.

✓ **Dental care**

There's nothing more frightening than having a toothache when you're far from home. Have a dental check-up before you leave on a long trip to avoid any problems.

✓ **Medications**

Talk to your doctor before your trip. Your doctor may be able to write a prescription for extra medication or give you tips for staying healthy while traveling. Buy and pack a supply of all medications you take regularly. Carry your medications in your carry-on bags. If you lose your luggage, you will still have them.

SOURCE: www.atevo.com

B ▸ **PAIR WORK.** In addition to medical items, what else should go on a checklist for an international trip? Write a list with your partner.

CHECKLIST

☑ _____

☑ _____

☑ _____

☑ _____

C 🎧 **SOUND BITES.** **Read along silently as you listen to two short conversations in Russia.**

GUEST: I need to see a dentist as soon as possible. I think it's an emergency. I was wondering if you might be able to recommend someone who speaks English.

CLERK: Actually, there's one not far from here. Would you like me to make an appointment for you?

DENTIST: So I hear you're from overseas.

PATIENT: Yes. From Venezuela. Thanks for fitting me in. This tooth is killing me.

DENTIST: Luckily, I had a cancellation. Glad to be of help.

PATIENT: I really appreciate it. Thought I'd better see someone right away.

DENTIST: Well, let's have a look.

D **Check the statements that you are sure are true.** **Explain your answers.**

☑ **1.** The hotel guest is having a dental emergency.

☐ **2.** The hotel guest is on vacation.

☑ **3.** The hotel clerk offers to call the dentist.

☐ **4.** It was easy to get an appointment with the dentist.

E **IN OTHER WORDS.** **Explain the meaning of each underlined phrase.**

I understand

1. "So I hear you're from overseas."

2. "Thanks for fitting me in."
   taking me in appointment

is hurts a lot

3. "This tooth is killing me."

4. "Well, let's have a look."
   let's check

WHAT ABOUT **YOU?**

Have you ever had a medical or dental emergency? Where were you? What happened? What did you do?

> ❝ Last year, I went skiing and I broke my arm. I had to go to the emergency room at the hospital. ❞

1 Make an Appointment to See a Dentist

🎧 CONVERSATION MODEL Read and listen.

A: Hello. I wonder if I might be able to see the dentist today. I'm here on business, and I have a toothache.

B: Oh, that must hurt. Are you in a lot of pain?

A: Yes, actually, I am.

B: Well, let me check. Could you be here by 3:00?

A: Yes. That would be fine. I really appreciate it.

🎧 **Rhythm and intonation practice**

A 🎧 **VOCABULARY.** Dental emergencies. **Listen and practice.**

I have a toothache.

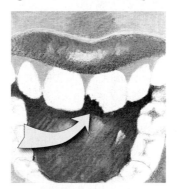

I broke a tooth.

I lost a filling.

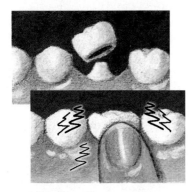

My crown is loose.

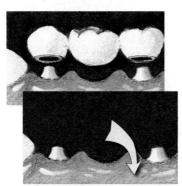

My bridge came out.

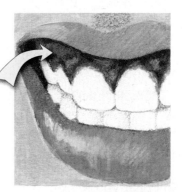

My gums are swollen.

B 🎧 **LISTENING COMPREHENSION.** **Listen to the conversations. Complete each statement to describe the dental problem.**

1. The man lost _____ .

2. The woman's _____ is loose.

3. The man's _____ came out.

4. The woman just broke _____ .

C **GRAMMAR.** Use <u>May</u>, <u>might</u>, <u>must</u>, and <u>be able to</u>

<u>May</u> or <u>might</u> for possibility
Use <u>may</u> or <u>might</u> and the base form to express possibility. They have the same meaning.
The dentist **may** (or **might**) **have** some time to see you.
Barbara **might** (or **may**) **not need** a new filling.

<u>Must</u> for conclusions *99% sure*
Use <u>must</u> and the base form of a verb when something is almost certainly true.
John just broke a tooth. That **must hurt**.
The dentist told me to come next week. It **must not be** an emergency.

phasal modal
<u>Be able to</u> for ability or possibility
<u>Be able to</u> has the same meaning as <u>can</u>.
She'**ll be able to see** you tomorrow. = She **can see** you tomorrow.

Note: You can use <u>be able to</u> or <u>have to</u> with <u>may</u>, <u>might</u>, or <u>must</u>.

Dr. Sharp	may	be able to	help you.
I	might not	be able to	get there till 6:00.
You	might	have to	get a new crown.
She	must not	have to	go to work today.

PAGE G3
For more ...

D **PAIR WORK.** Discuss the questions. Use <u>may</u> or <u>might</u>.

1. When will you practice English outside class this week?

2. When will you need to use English in your life?

E Complete the conversations by drawing conclusions with <u>must</u> or <u>must not</u>.

1. **A:** You look terrible! Your tooth _must_ really hurt.
   B: It does.

2. **A:** Did you call the dentist?
   B: Yes, but no one is answering. The dentist _must not_ be in today.

3. **A:** Bill had a bad toothache this morning.
   B: No kidding. Then he _must not_ be able to come to the meeting today.

4. **A:** Where's Alice?
   B: Well, I heard she lost a filling, so she _must_ be at the dentist.

CONVERSATION
PAIR WORK

Role-play making an appointment to see a dentist. Start like this:

A: Hello. I wonder if I might be able to see the dentist today. _____ .

B: _____ ...

CONTROLLED PRACTICE

Describe Symptoms at a Doctor's Office

CONVERSATION MODEL Read and listen.

A: You must be Mr. Brown. You're here for a blood test, aren't you?
B: That's right.
A: And is anything bothering you today?
B: Well, actually, I've been coughing.
A: Really? Well, why don't you have a seat? I'll see if the doctor can see you.

Rhythm and intonation practice

A **VOCABULARY.** Symptoms. **Listen and practice.**

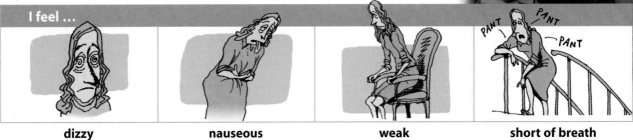

I feel ...
dizzy   nauseous   weak   short of breath

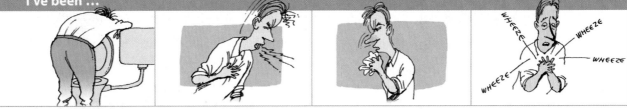

I've been ...
vomiting   coughing   sneezing   wheezing

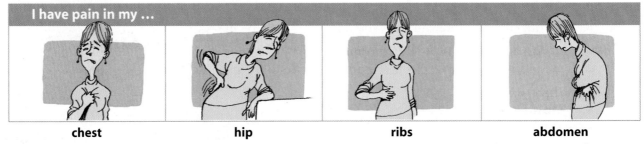

I have pain in my ...
chest   hip   ribs   abdomen

B **PRONUNCIATION.** Intonation of lists. **Listen. Then listen again and repeat.**

1. I feel **weak** and **dizzy**.

2. I've been **sneezing**, **coughing**, and **wheezing**.

3. I have pain in **my neck**, **my shoulders**, **my back**, and **my hip**.

🎧 **LISTENING COMPREHENSION.** **Listen to the conversations. Check the symptoms each patient describes. If the patient has any pain, where is it? Listen again to check your work.**

	dizziness	nausea	weakness	vomiting	coughing	sneezing	wheezing	pain	if pain, where?
1.	☑	☐	☑	☐	☐	☐	☐	☑	shoulder
2.	☐	☐	☐	☐	☑	☐	☐	☑	back neck
3.	☐	☐	☐	☐	☐	☑	☐	☑	back
4.	☐	☑	☐	☑	☐	☐	☐	☐	
5.	☐	☐	☐	☐	☐	☐	☑	☐	
6.	☐	☐	☐	☐	☐	☐	☐	☑	hip

D 🎧 **VOCABULARY.** Medical procedures. **Listen and practice.**

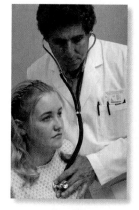
a checkup /
an examination

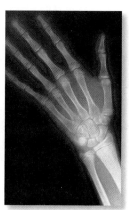
an X-ray

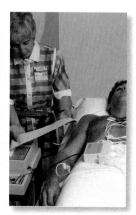
an EKG

a shot /
an injection

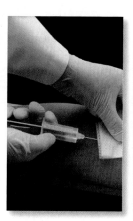
a blood test

CONVERSATION
PAIR WORK

Role-play a visit to the doctor's office. Before you begin, choose a time and medical procedure and write it in the appointment book. Use the guide, or create a new conversation.

A: You must be _____ . You're here for _____ , aren't you?

B: _____ .

A: And is anything bothering you today?

B: Well, actually, _____ .

A: _____ .

APPOINTMENTS		
	patient's name	medical procedure
8:00		
9:00		
10:00		
11:00		
12:00		
1:00		
2:00		
3:00		
4:00		
5:00		
6:00		
7:00		

3 Discuss Types of Medical Treatments

A **READING WARM-UP.** What do you do when you get sick or you're in pain?

B 🎧 **READING.** Read the article. Which health treatments have you tried?

CONVENTIONAL MEDICINE

The beginnings of conventional medicine can be traced back to the fifth century B.C. in ancient Greece. It is based on the scientific study of the human body and illness. In the last century, there has been great progress in what doctors have been able to do with modern surgery and new medications. These scientific advances have made conventional medicine the method many people choose first when they need medical help.

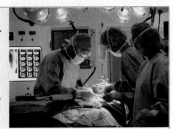
Surgical techniques have greatly improved over the last century.

HOMEOPATHY

Homeopathic remedies are popular in many countries.

Homeopathy was founded in the late eighteenth century in Germany. It is a low-cost system of natural medicine used by hundreds of millions of people worldwide, particularly in India, France, Germany, and the United Kingdom. Homeopathic remedies always come from plants and other natural sources, and they are designed to try to get the body to heal itself. The remedies are usually taken under the tongue.

HERBAL THERAPY

Herbal medicine, often taken as teas or pills, has been practiced for thousands of years in almost all cultures around the world. In fact, many conventional medicines were discovered by scientists studying traditional uses of herbs for medicinal purposes. The World Health Organization claims that 80% of the world's population uses some form of herbal therapy for their regular health care.

Herbs are used to treat many ailments.

ACUPUNCTURE

An acupuncturist inserts needles at certain points on the body.

Acupuncture originated in China over five thousand years ago. Today, it is used worldwide for a variety of problems. Acupuncture needles are inserted at certain points on the body to relieve pain and/or restore health. Many believe acupuncture may be effective in helping people stop smoking as well.

CHIROPRACTIC

Chiropractic was introduced in the U.S. in 1895 and is now used by 15 million people worldwide for the treatment of pain, backache, injuries and some illnesses. Chiropractic uses no medications, but it is sometimes practiced along with herbal or homeopathic therapies.

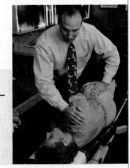
A chiropractor adjusts a patient's spine.

SPIRITUAL HEALING

Many believe meditation or prayer may help heal disease.

Also known as faith healing, or mind and body connection, various forms of spiritual healing exist around the world. This is a form of healing that uses the mind or religious faith to treat illness. A number of conventional doctors even say that when they have not been able to help a patient, spiritual healing just may work.

SOURCES: www.alternativemedicine.com and www.holisticmed.com

DISCUSSION. Which of the treatments in the reading are available
in your country? Which ones are the most popular? Why?

WHAT DO YOU THINK? Match each patient to a treatment. Explain
your answers. In some cases, more than one therapy might be appropriate.

1. ❝I want to avoid taking
any strong medications
or having surgery.❞

This patient might prefer
_____.

2. ❝I believe you have to
heal yourself. You can't
just expect doctors to do
everything for you.❞

This patient might prefer
_____.

3. ❝I wouldn't use a health
care method that isn't strongly
supported by scientific
research.❞

This patient might prefer
_____.

TOP NOTCH
INTERACTION • *What works for you?*

Practitioners
a conventional doctor
a homeopathic doctor
an acupuncturist
an herbal therapist
a chiropractor
a spiritual healer

STEP 1. PAIR WORK. Discuss the medical treatments and practitioners
you would choose for each ailment. Take notes on your notepad.

	You	Your partner
a cold		
a headache		
nausea		
back pain		
a high fever		
a broken finger		

STEP 2. DISCUSSION. Compare the kinds of health care you and your
classmates use. Explain why you use them.

❝I've tried acupuncture a
number of times. It really
helped with my back pain.❞

❝I would never try herbal
medicine. I don't think
it works.❞

❝I see a homeopathic doctor
regularly, but my husband
doesn't believe in that.❞

STEP 3. WRITING. On a separate sheet of paper, write about the health care you use.

4 *Talk about Medications*

Medicine label information
Dosage: Take 1 tablet by mouth every day.
Warnings: Do not take this medication if you are pregnant or nursing a baby.
Side effects: May cause dizziness or nausea.

A 🎧 **VOCABULARY.** Medications.
Listen and practice.

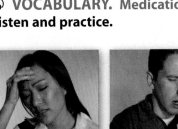
a painkiller

cold tablets

a nasal spray /
a decongestant

eye drops

an antihistamine

cough medicine

an antibiotic

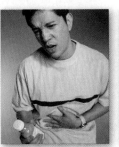
an antacid

an ointment

vitamins

B 🎧 **LISTENING COMPREHENSION.**
Listen to each patient talk with a
doctor. Use the vocabulary to fill
out the chart for each patient.

NAME: _Valerie Ramazan_

	NO	YES	
Is the patient currently taking any medication?	☐	☐	If so, which type? _____
Are there any possible side effects?	☐	☐	If so, what are they? _____
Did the doctor give the patient a prescription?	☐	☐	

NAME: _Lucy Fernandez_

	NO	YES	
Is the patient currently taking any medication?	☐	☐	If so, which type? _____
Are there any possible side effects?	☐	☐	If so, what are they? _____
Did the doctor give the patient a prescription?	☐	☐	

NAME: _____ **Mark Goh** _____

	NO	YES	
Is the patient currently taking any medication?	☐	☐	If so, which type? _____
Are there any possible side effects?	☐	☐	If so, what are they? _____
Did the doctor give the patient a prescription?	☐	☐	

INTERACTION • *Are you currently taking any medication?*

STEP 1. **Imagine you are visiting the doctor. Complete the patient information form.**

Patient Information Form

NAME: _____

1. What are your symptoms?
   - ☐ dizziness
   - ☐ coughing
   - ☐ nausea
   - ☐ weakness
   - ☐ sneezing
   - ☐ vomiting
   - ☐ shortness of breath
   - ☐ wheezing
   - ☐ pain (where? _____)
   - ☐ other: _____

2. How long have you had these symptoms? _____

3. Are you currently taking any medications?
   If so, what? _____

4. Are you allergic to any medications?
   If so, which? _____

STEP 2. **ROLE PLAY. Take turns playing different roles. Use your patient information form. Include the following scenes:**

Roles
a patient
a colleague / classmate
a doctor
a receptionist

1. The colleague or classmate recommends a doctor.
2. The patient calls the receptionist to make an appointment.
3. The receptionist greets the patient at the office.
4. The doctor asks about the problem and suggests a treatment.

NEED HELP? **Here's language you already know:**

Finding a doctor

Could you recommend ___?

I'd like to make an appointment to see ___.

I think it's an emergency.

I really appreciate it.

At the doctor's office

Is it an emergency?

Why don't you have a seat?

You must be ___.

I'll see if the doctor can see you.

The doctor will be right with you.

The doctor

Luckily, I had a cancellation.

Glad I'm able to help you out.

It's a good idea to ___.

You should ___.

You may have to ___.

Let's have a look.

That must hurt.

The patient

Thanks for fitting me in.

My ___ is killing me.

I feel [dizzy].

I've been [coughing].

I have pain in my [ankle].

I thought I'd better see someone right away.

Are there any side effects?

A 🎧 **LISTENING COMPREHENSION.** **Listen to the conversations. Complete the statements.**

1. The patient lost a _____ .

2. The doctor wrote a prescription for an _____ .

3. The doctor wants the patient to get an _____ .

4. The patient wants to see an _____ .

B **Suggest a medication for each of the people.**

1. _____   2. _____   3. _____   4. _____   5. _____   6. _____

C **Complete each conversation with a statement using <u>must</u>.**

1. **A:** I feel weak and dizzy, and I've been vomiting all morning.
   B: You ___*must feel terrible*___ .

2. **A:** My brother stayed up all night dancing. He got home at 7:00 A.M.
   B: He _____ .

3. **A:** I tried to make an appointment with a dentist, but they can't fit me in this week.
   B: They _____ .

4. **A:** My daughter is getting married next week.
   B: You _____ .

D **Rewrite each statement, using <u>may</u> (or <u>might</u>) and <u>be able to</u>.**

1. Maybe the doctor can see you tomorrow.
   ___The doctor might be able to see you tomorrow.___

2. Maybe an acupuncturist can help you.
   _____

3. Maybe the hotel can recommend a good dentist.
   _____

4. Maybe she can't come to the office before 6:00.
   _____

5. Maybe you can buy an antihistamine in the gift shop.
   _____

TOP NOTCH **PROJECT**
Use a bilingual dictionary to make a list of more medical and dental vocabulary.

TOP NOTCH **WEBSITE**
For Unit 2 online activities, visit the *Top Notch* Companion Website at www.longman.com/topnotch.

UNIT WRAP-UP

- **Vocabulary.** Name all the treatments, procedures, and ailments you can see in the picture.
  backache, X-ray, ...

- **Grammar.** Make statements with <u>may</u> or <u>might</u> and <u>must</u>.
  She must have a backache.

- **Social Language.** Create conversations for the people.
  A: I wonder if I might be able to see the dentist today.
  B: Is it an emergency?

- **Writing.** Write about what is happening in the picture.
  The medical office is very busy today. There are a lot of...

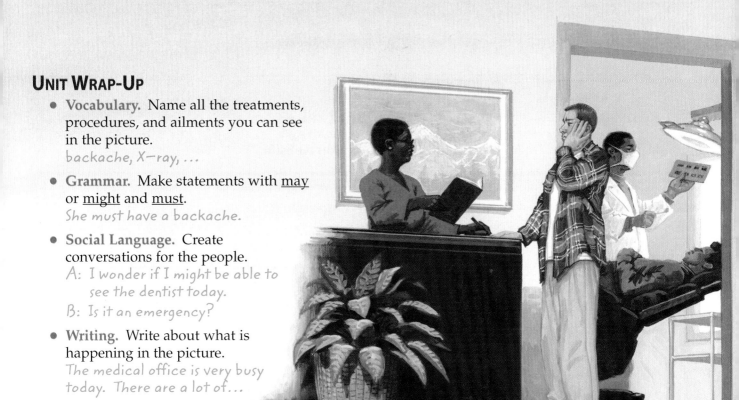

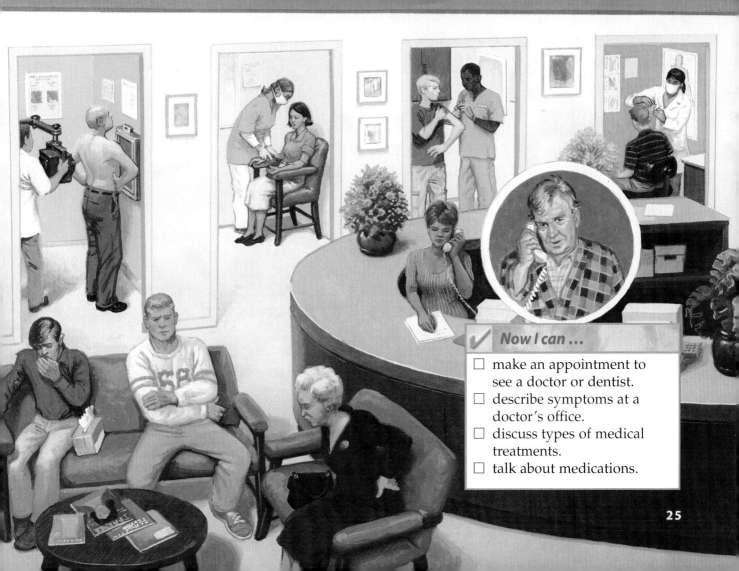

✔ Now I can ...

- ☐ make an appointment to see a doctor or dentist.
- ☐ describe symptoms at a doctor's office.
- ☐ discuss types of medical treatments.
- ☐ talk about medications.

Getting Things Done

UNIT GOALS
1 Request express service
2 Ask for a recommendation
3 Evaluate the quality of service
4 Plan a social event

A TOPIC PREVIEW. Look at the business services website.

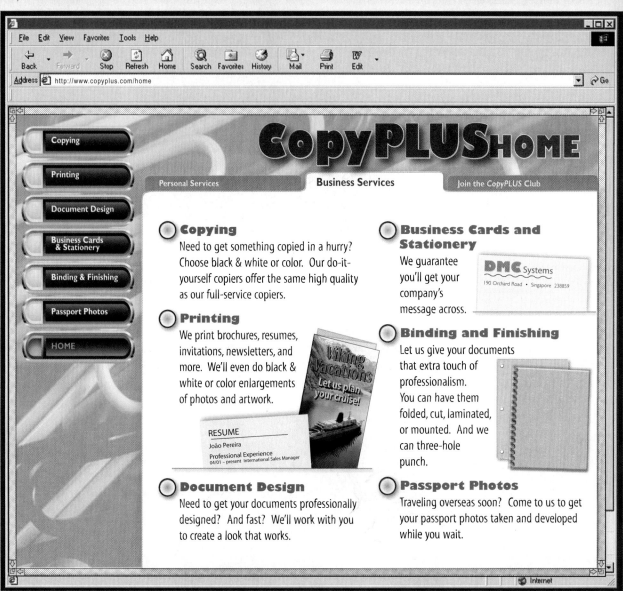

B DISCUSSION. When might you need each of these services? Give examples.

> If I started my own business, I might want to print some brochures.

> If I travel overseas, I'll need a passport.

SUE: You look like you're in a hurry!

KIM: I am. I've got to get 50 color copies made a.s.a.p.* I hope they can do a rush job.

SUE: They must get requests like that all the time.

KIM: I sure hope so. But that's not all.

SUE: What else?

*a.s.a.p. = as soon as possible

KIM: Then I've got to get it all air expressed so it arrives in Singapore first thing Monday morning.

SUE: I won't keep you then. Actually, I'm in a bit of a hurry myself. I need to have the tailor put new buttons on this jacket.

KIM: OK. I'll call you tonight.

SUE: Great!

D **IN OTHER WORDS.** Read the conversation again and restate the following underlined words and phrases in your <u>own</u> way.

1. You look like you're <u>in a hurry</u>.
2. I hope they can <u>do a rush job</u>.
3. <u>first thing</u> Monday morning
4. I <u>won't keep you</u> then.

WHAT ABOUT **YOU?**

PAIR WORK. Which business and non-business services have you used in the last year? Who was the service provider? Which other services have you used?

☐ copying

☐ printing

☐ housecleaning

☐ car repair

☐ tailoring

☐ courier service

Request Express Service

 CONVERSATION
MODEL Read and listen.

A: Do you think I could get this dry-cleaned by Thursday?

B: Thursday? That might be difficult.

A: I'm sorry, but it's pretty urgent. I need it for a friend's wedding this weekend.

B: Well, in that case, I'll see what I can do. But it won't be ready until after four o'clock.

A: I really appreciate it. Thanks.

 Rhythm and intonation practice

A **VOCABULARY. Services. Listen and practice.**

dry-clean a suit

develop / process film

repair shoes

frame a picture

deliver a package

lengthen / shorten a skirt

enlarge photos

print a sign

copy a report

B ▸ GRAMMAR. The passive causative

Use <u>get</u> or <u>have</u> with an object and the past participle to talk about arranging services.
<u>Get</u> and <u>have</u> have the same meaning in the passive causative.

	get / have	object	past participle	
They	got	their vacation photos	enlarged.	
I need to	get	this report	copied.	
We	're having	the office	cleaned	tomorrow.
She can	have	her film	developed	in an hour.

A <u>by</u> phrase is used when the speaker thinks that information is important.
We're having the office cleaned **by Royal Cleaning Services**.
They got the copier repaired yesterday. (no <u>by</u> phrase; not necessary to know by whom)

GRAMMAR BOOSTER
PAGE G4
For more …

C ▸ 🎧 LISTENING COMPREHENSION. Listen to the conversations.
Complete each statement with the item and a service.

1. He wants to get his _____ _____ .
2. She needs to get her _____ _____ .
3. He needs to have his _____ _____ .
4. She wants to have a _____ _____ .

D ▸ Use the cues to write questions with the passive causative.

1. Would it be possible to / these pictures / frame / by next week? _____
2. Could I / these shoes / repair / here? _____
3. Can I / this shirt / dry-clean / by tomorrow? _____
4. Where can I / these gloves / gift wrap? _____
5. Is it possible to / these photos / enlarge / before 5:00? _____

E ▸ PAIR WORK. Where do you go for these services? Use the passive causative.

dry-clean clothes   cut hair   process film   make photocopies

repair shoes

❝Where do you get your clothes dry-cleaned?❞

❝I usually get them dry-cleaned at …❞

CONVERSATION PAIR WORK

Role-play asking for express service.

A: Do you think I could _____ by _____?
B: _____? That might be difficult.
A: _____ …

Continue the conversation in your <u>own</u> way.

Ideas for why you might be in a rush:
for a wedding
for a business trip
for a vacation
for a new job

CONTROLLED PRACTICE

2 ▸ Ask for a Recommendation

🎧 CONVERSATION MODEL Read and listen.

A: I have to get this to Chicago a.s.a.p. Can you recommend a courier service?

B: Why don't you have Aero Flash take care of it?

A: Have you used them before?

B: Sure. They're really reliable. And they can deliver a package anywhere in the world in two business days.

🎧 **Rhythm and intonation practice**

A **GRAMMAR.** Causatives <u>get</u>, <u>have</u>, and <u>make</u> + Let

Use the causative to show that one person causes another person to do something.
With <u>get</u>, use an object and an infinitive. With <u>have</u>, use an object and a base form of a verb.

		object	**infinitive**	
I	got	my brother	to help	me finish the job.

		object	**base form**	
She	had	her assistant	plan	the meeting.

To suggest an <u>obligation</u>, use <u>make</u> with an object and a base form.
I made my brother help me finish the job.

GRAMMAR BOOSTER

PAGES G4–G5
For more …

B **Correct the error in each sentence.**

1. Why don't you have your assistant ~~to~~ call them?

2. Why didn't you get your sister ~~help~~ you? *to help*

3. I'll never be able to get the dry cleaner ~~do~~ this by tomorrow! *to do*

4. You should have the hotel ~~to~~ give you your money back. *give*

5. Why don't you make your brother ~~to~~ wash the dishes? *wash*

6. I'm sure we can get the store ~~process~~ the film in an hour. *to process*

C 🎧 **VOCABULARY.** Adjectives to describe services. **Listen and practice.**

reliable   can be trusted to keep a promise
reasonable   doesn't charge too much money
fast   does the job in a short time
honest   does not lie or cheat
efficient   doesn't waste time
helpful   is willing to help
professional   does a very good job

D **PRONUNCIATION.** Emphatic stress to express enthusiasm. **Listen and repeat.**

1. They're **REAL**ly reliable.
2. They're in**CRED**ibly fast.
3. He's ex**TREME**ly helpful.
4. She's **SO** professional.

E **Circle the best adjective for each situation.**

1. "Link Copy Service was so (reasonable / helpful / honest). They delivered the job to my office before I had to leave for the airport."

2. "I find Portello's to be extremely (professional / fast / reasonable). I've shopped around and I can't find another service with such low prices."

3. "If you're looking for a good housecleaning service, I'd recommend Citywide Services. They're incredibly (efficient / reliable / honest). They have two people working together to complete the job in no time at all."

4. "What I like about Dom's Auto Service is that they're so (fast / reasonable / honest). There are so many other places that you can't trust. But at Dom's they always tell you the truth."

CONVERSATION
PAIR WORK

Role-play asking for a recommendation. Use the guide and the ads, or create your own conversation.

A: I have to _____ a.s.a.p. Can you recommend a _____?
B: Why don't you have _____ take care of it?
A: Have you used them before?
B: _____ …

Continue the conversation in your own way.

Ideas:

You need someone to make 200 color copies of a report.

You need someone to send a package to Moscow.

You need someone to dry-clean your suit / dress / jacket before an important meeting.

You need someone to service your car before a long trip.

a copy service

a courier service

a dry cleaner

an auto repair shop

Evaluate the Quality of Service

A **READING WARM-UP.** Have you ever bought handmade clothing or other handmade things? Do you prefer handmade or factory-made?

B 🎧 **READING.** Read the tourist information for visitors to Hong Kong. Are there services like these in your city or town?

PLACES TO SHOP

HONG KONG TAILORS

The famous Hong Kong 24-hour suit is a thing of the past, but you can still have clothes custom-made in a few days. Today, prices are no longer as low as they once were, but they're often about what you'd pay for a ready-made garment back home; the difference, of course, is that a tailor-made garment should fit you perfectly. The workmanship and quality of the better established shops rival even those of London's Savile Row—at less than half the price. A top-quality men's suit will run about HK$7,000 (US$910) or more, including fabric, while a silk shirt can cost HK$600 (US$78).

Tailors in Hong Kong will make almost any garment you want—suits, evening gowns, wedding dresses, leather jackets, even monogrammed shirts. Many tailors offer a wide range of cloth from which to choose, from cotton and linen to very fine wools, cashmere, and silk. Hong Kong tailors are excellent at copying fashions. Bring a picture or drawing of what you want.

You should allow three to five days to have a garment custom-made, with at least two or three fittings. If you aren't satisfied during the fittings,

You can choose from a variety of fabrics.

linen
cotton
wool
cashmere
silk

At your first fitting, the tailor will take your measurements. At your next fitting, the tailor will make alterations until you're satisfied.

speak up. Alterations should be included in the original price. If, in the end, you still don't like the finished product, you don't have to accept it. However, you will forfeit the deposit you are required to pay before the tailor begins working, usually about 50% of the total cost.

With more than 2,500 tailoring establishments in Hong Kong, it shouldn't be any problem finding one. Some of the most famous are located in hotel shopping arcades and shopping complexes, but the more upscale the location, the higher the prices.

Once you've had something custom-made and your tailor has your measurements, you will more than likely be able to order additional clothing later, even after you've returned home!

You can get anything made—from an evening gown to a monogrammed shirt.

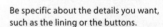

Be specific about the details you want, such as the lining or the buttons.

SOURCE: *Frommer's Hong Kong*, 7th edition

C ▸ **PAIR WORK.** **Check the statements that are true, according to the article. Find the information to support your answers in the reading.**

☐ **1.** You used to be able to get a suit made in 24 hours in Hong Kong.

☐ **2.** If you buy a ready-made garment at a store at home, it will cost about the same as a custom-made garment in Hong Kong.

☐ **3.** If you get a garment made on Savile Row, you will pay about 50 percent less than you would pay for the same garment made in Hong Kong.

☐ **4.** If you don't like the garment you ordered, you can get all your money back.

☐ **5.** If you want to pay a low price for a custom-made garment, go to an upscale hotel shopping arcade.

D ▸ **DISCUSSION.** **Do you think the Hong Kong tailoring services described in the tour guide sound like "a good deal"? What's more important to you—price or quality?**

TOP NOTCH
INTERACTION • *They're the best!*

STEP 1. **What services do you use? Complete the chart. Write the name of the business, and check the reasons why you use that service. Then compare your chart with your partner's.**

	name of business	speed	reliability	price	workmanship	location
dry cleaning		☐	☐	☐	☐	☐
photo processing		☐	☐	☐	☐	☐
auto repair		☐	☐	☐	☐	☐
bicycle repair		☐	☐	☐	☐	☐
tailoring		☐	☐	☐	☐	☐
express delivery		☐	☐	☐	☐	☐
shoe repair		☐	☐	☐	☐	☐
hair stylist		☐	☐	☐	☐	☐
other:		☐	☐	☐	☐	☐

STEP 2. DISCUSSION. **Recommend local businesses to your classmates. Explain why you use them.**

> ❝I always get my clothes dry-cleaned at Royal Dry Cleaners on 45th Road. They're really fast, and the prices are quite reasonable.❞

STEP 3. WRITING. **Write an advertisement for a local service that you use and like. Describe the quality of the service and the workmanship.**

4 ▷ *Plan a Social Event*

A 🎧 **VOCABULARY.** Steps for planning a social event. **Listen and practice.**

make a guest list

pick a date, time, and place

make a budget

assign responsibilities

send out invitations

call a caterer

hire a DJ

decorate the room

B 🎧 **LISTENING COMPREHENSION.** Listen to the conversation. Number the steps in order. Then listen again and check who will do each step.

	She'll do it herself.	She'll get help.
____ make a guest list	☐	☐
____ pick a date and time	☐	☐
____ pick a place	☐	☐
____ make a budget	☐	☐
____ assign responsibilities	☐	☐
____ send out invitations	☐	☐
____ call a caterer	☐	☐
____ hire a DJ	☐	☐
____ decorate the room	☐	☐

STEP 1. Take the survey. Compare your answers with a partner's.

What kind of
personality
do you have?

Priscila

Check which activities you would rather do.
Choose from column A or column B.

Column A		Column B
⊗ spend money	or	◯ plan a budget
◯ assign responsibility	or	⊗ take responsibility
◯ design invitations	or	⊗ send invitations
◯ play your own music	or	⊗ hire a DJ
⊗ decorate a room	or	◯ make a guest list
⊗ bring your own food	or	◯ call a caterer
⊗ dance	or	◯ watch other people dance
◯ sing	or	⊗ listen to other people sing
◯ hire someone to clean	or	⊗ clean up after a party

If you chose:

five or more from column A,
you're the wild and creative type! You'd be a lot of fun at a party!

five or more from column B,
you're a born leader! You could plan a great party!

about the same from each column,
you're the best of both worlds!

Some ideas:

An end-of-year party? A birthday party? A TGIF* party?

*Thank Goodness It's Friday!

A talent show? A karaoke party?

An English practice day?

STEP 2. GROUP WORK. Plan a social event for your class. Choose a type of event and discuss the steps you would need to take. Write the actions in your notepad.

Type of event:	
Steps:	

A 🎧 **LISTENING COMPREHENSION. Listen to each conversation. Write a sentence to describe what the customer needs and when.**

1. *She needs to get her dress dry-cleaned by Friday.*

2. _____

3. _____

4. _____

B **Complete each statement or question with a noun. Use your <u>own</u> words.**

1. Can I get my _____ dry-cleaned here?

2. I'd like to have these _____ lengthened.

3. Where can I get these _____ shortened?

4. Can you tell me where I can get some _____ copied?

5. Where did she get her _____ framed?

6. How much did he pay to have his _____ repaired?

7. I need to get some _____ printed.

8. I'm in a hurry to have my _____ processed.

C **Complete each causative statement in your <u>own</u> way. Begin with the base form of a verb or an infinitive.**

1. I got the teacher *to help me with my writing* .

2. At the end of the meal, I had the waiter _____ .

3. Before my last vacation, I got the travel agent _____ .

4. When I was young, my mother always made me _____ .

5. When you arrive, you should get the hotel _____ .

6. Don't forget to have the gas station attendant _____ .

7. If you come for dinner, I promise I won't make you _____ .

8. Sad movies always make me _____ .

9. Maybe you can get your friend _____ .

10. You should have Air Express Courier Service _____ .

D **WRITING. What kinds of services are difficult to find? Write about the services you would like to have in your neighborhood.**

> *TOP NOTCH* **SONG**
> "I'll Get Back to You"
> Lyrics on last page before Workbook.

> *TOP NOTCH* **PROJECT**
> Have a real social event for the class. Invite other classes to join you.

> *TOP NOTCH* **WEBSITE**
> For Unit 3 online activities, visit the *Top Notch* Companion Website at www.longman.com/topnotch.

UNIT WRAP-UP

- **Social Language.** Create conversations for the people.
  I've got to get this to Los Angeles a.s.a.p.

- **Grammar.** Use the passive causative to describe the services the man wants or needs.

- **Writing.** Tell the story of the man's day.

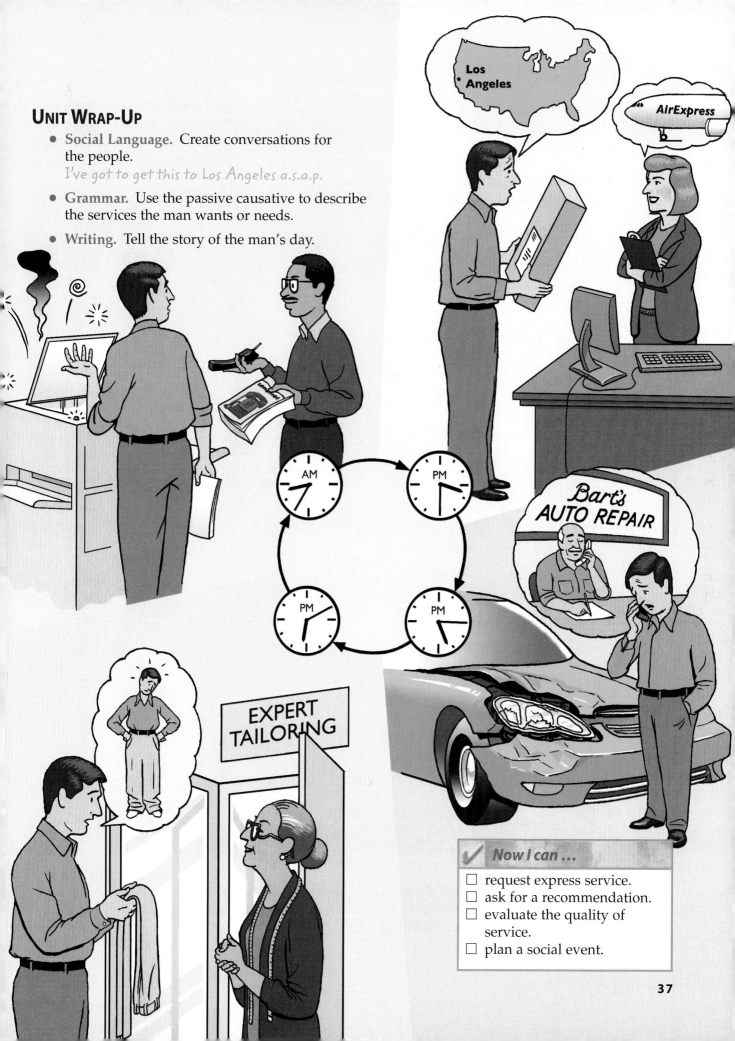

Los Angeles

AirExpress

Bart's AUTO REPAIR

EXPERT TAILORING

✓ Now I can ...

- ☐ request express service.
- ☐ ask for a recommendation.
- ☐ evaluate the quality of service.
- ☐ plan a social event.

37

Life Choices

UNIT GOALS

1 Explain a change in life and work choice
2 Express regrets about decisions
3 Discuss skills, abilities, and qualification:
4 Discuss work and life decisions

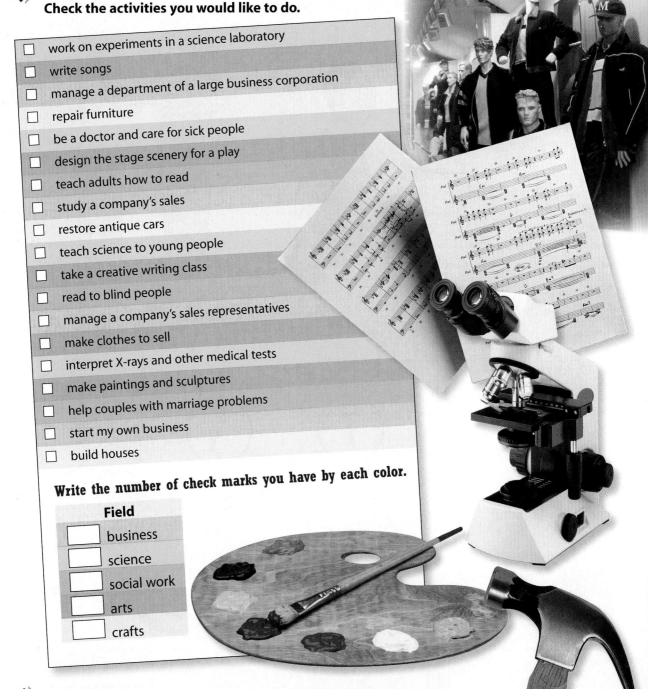

A▸ TOPIC PREVIEW. Take the work preference inventory. Check the activities you would like to do.

- ☐ work on experiments in a science laboratory
- ☐ write songs
- ☐ manage a department of a large business corporation
- ☐ repair furniture
- ☐ be a doctor and care for sick people
- ☐ design the stage scenery for a play
- ☐ teach adults how to read
- ☐ study a company's sales
- ☐ restore antique cars
- ☐ teach science to young people
- ☐ take a creative writing class
- ☐ read to blind people
- ☐ manage a company's sales representatives
- ☐ make clothes to sell
- ☐ interpret X-rays and other medical tests
- ☐ make paintings and sculptures
- ☐ help couples with marriage problems
- ☐ start my own business
- ☐ build houses

Write the number of check marks you have by each color.

Field
- ☐ business
- ☐ science
- ☐ social work
- ☐ arts
- ☐ crafts

B▸ DISCUSSION. Which field did you have the most check marks for? What are some jobs in that field? Do you have a job in that field now? Would you like to? Is that job the same job you wanted when you were younger?

C 🎧 **SOUND BITES.** Read along silently as you listen to a natural conversation.

ANN: Ruth! This report's due tomorrow. What are you dreaming about?

RUTH: You know, I wish I'd gone to medical school instead of business school.

ANN: What? Since when have you been interested in medicine?

RUTH: Well, when I read about doctor shortages and terrible diseases, I think about how I could have made a difference in this world, an important difference… instead of doing these useless reports!

ANN: Well, you're young. Maybe it's not too late.

RUTH: Think so?

ANN: Sure. But do you think maybe you could get your head out of the clouds and get back on task now?

RUTH: Sorry about that. You can count on me.

D Check the statements that are true.

☐ **1.** Ann is surprised to hear about Ruth's interest in medicine.
☐ **2.** Ruth thinks business is more useful than medicine.
☐ **3.** Ruth would like to be a doctor.
☐ **4.** Ann suggests that it's possible for Ruth to change careers.

E **IN OTHER WORDS.** With a partner, restate each of the following statements in another way.

1. "I could have made a difference in this world…"

2. "Maybe it's not too late."

3. "…could [you] get your head out of the clouds and get back on task now?"

4. "You can count on me."

WHAT ABOUT **YOU?**

What regrets do you have in your life? What decisions do you wish you could change?

☐ a job choice
☐ a job change

☐ your studies
☐ your marriage / divorce

☐ a friendship that ended
☐ other: _____

1 ▷ *Explain a Change in Life and Work Choices*

🎧 CONVERSATION MODEL Read and listen.

A: Hey, Art! Long time no see.

B: Ben! How have you been?

A: Not bad, thanks. So what are you doing these days?

B: Well, I'm in dental school.

A: No kidding! I thought you had other plans.

B: That's right. I was going to be an artist, but I changed my mind.

A: How come? *= hard to make money*

B: Well, it's <u>hard to make a living as a painter!</u>

🎧 **Rhythm and intonation practice**

Ⓐ GRAMMAR. Future in the past: <u>was</u> / <u>were going to</u> and <u>would</u>

Use <u>was</u> / <u>were going to</u> + the base form of a verb to express future plans someone had in the past.

I **was going to get** married, but I changed my mind.
I believed I **was going to have** a lot of children, but I was wrong.

Weren't you **going to study** law?	Yes, I was. / No, I wasn't.
Who **was going to teach** this class?	My sister was.
Where **were they going to study**?	In Prague.

<u>Would</u> + the base form of the verb can also express future in the past, but only after statements of knowledge or belief.   *If would*

She (thought) she **would be** a doctor, but she changed her mind.
We always (believed) they **would get** married, but they never did.

PAGES G5–G7
For more ...

Ⓑ Read each person's New Year's resolution from January 2000, the turn of the century. Write what each person was going to do.

Ivan Potok

Marie Duclos

Sylvia Strook

Robert Park

"I'm going to stop smoking."

Ivan was going to
stop smoking.

"I'm going to apply to law school."

_____

_____

"I'm going to find a husband."

_____

_____

"I'm going to marry Sylvia Strook."

_____

_____

C Use the cues to make statements with <u>would</u>.

1. In 1990 Sam thought / be / a lawyer, but he decided against it.
2. When I was young, I believed / study Chinese, but I never did.
3. Everyone was sure / Bill and Stella / get a divorce, but they didn't!
4. We didn't know / we / have so many children, but now we have six!

D DISCUSSION. **Compare the plans and beliefs you had about your own future when you were young.**

> 66 When I was young, I thought I would be a teacher. 99

> 66 That's amazing! I thought I was going to be a teacher too, but I changed my mind. 99

E 🎧 VOCABULARY. **Reasons for changing your mind. Listen and practice.**

| I wanted to be a rock star, but **my tastes changed**. | I was going to be an artist, but **it's hard to make a living as an artist**. | I thought I would be a lawyer, but **I didn't pass the exam**. | I wanted to be a firefighter, but **my family talked me out of it**. | I was going to marry George, but **I just changed my mind**. |

ทัศน์ = in to it

F 🎧 LISTENING COMPREHENSION. **Listen to the conversations. Then listen again. Write the reason each person changed his or her mind.**

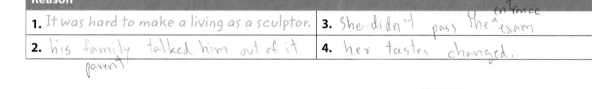

Reason	
1. It was hard to make a living as a sculptor.	3. She didn't pass the *entrance* ^exam
2. his family talked him out of it *parents*	4. her tastes changed.

CONVERSATION
PAIR WORK

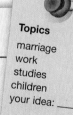

Topics
marriage
work
studies
children
your idea: _____

Role-play meeting someone you haven't seen for a while. Talk about changes in your life plans. Use the speech balloons and the topics for ideas.

> 66 Long time no see! 99

> 66 So what are you doing these days? 99

> 66 How have you been? 99

> 66 I was going to _____, but I changed my mind. 99

> 66 How come? 99

> 66 Well, _____. 99

41

CONTROLLED PRACTICE

2 *Express Regrets about Decisions*

🎧 CONVERSATION MODEL Read and listen.

A: I should have married Steven.

B: Why do you think that?

A: Well, I might have had children by now.

B: Could be. But you never know. You might not have been happy.

A: True.

🎧 Rhythm and intonation practice

A GRAMMAR. Perfect modals: meaning and form

Express regrets about past actions with <u>should have</u> and a past participle.

I **should have studied** medicine. (But unfortunately, I didn't.)

She **shouldn't have divorced** Sam. (But unfortunately, she did.)

Speculate about the past with <u>would have</u>, <u>could have</u>, <u>may have</u>, and <u>might have</u>, and a past participle.

I should have married her. We **would have been** happy.

He **could have made** a better career choice.

I **may have failed** the entrance exam. It was very hard.

He **may** (or **might**) not **have been** able to make a living as a painter.

Draw conclusions about the past with <u>must have</u> and a past participle.

He's not here. He **must have gone** home early. (Probably—but I don't know for sure.)

They didn't buy the house. The price **must not have been** acceptable. (Probably—but I don't know for sure.)

GRAMMAR BOOSTER

PAGE G7
For more …

B PAIR WORK. Share your regrets.

Partner A: Tell your partner what you regret about your life, your studies, your work, or your actions in the past. Use <u>should have</u> or <u>shouldn't have</u>.

Partner B: Ask why or why not.

C 🎧 **PRONUNCIATION.** Reduction of <u>have</u> in perfect modals. **Listen to the reduction of <u>have</u> in perfect modals. Then repeat.**

/ʃʊt̬əv/
1. I should have married Marie.

/maɪt̬əv/
2. They might have left.

/nɑt̬əv/
3. We may not have seen it.

/cʊt̬əv/
4. She could have been on time.

D **PAIR WORK.** **Provide reasons for each of the following statements.**
Partner A: Speculate with <u>may have</u> / <u>may not have</u> or <u>might have</u> / <u>might not have</u>.
Partner B: Draw a conclusion with <u>must have</u> or <u>must not have</u>.

Example: John is late for dinner.

He

1. My brother stopped studying English.
2. Claire left her husband.
3. Glen is 40, and he just got married.
4. They canceled the English class.
5. All the students failed the exam.

> 66 He may have gotten stuck in traffic. 99
>
> 66 He must have forgotten. 99

CONVERSATION
PAIR WORK

Express more regrets with your partner. Use the guide and the ideas from the box, or create a new conversation.

A: I should have _____ .
B: Why do you think that?
A: Well, I might have _____ .
B: Could be. But you never know.
You might _____ …

Continue the conversation in your <u>own</u> way.

💡 **Some ideas…**
- **taken a job [at Microsoft]**
- **bought a [sports car]**
- **studied [medicine]**
- **married [Pat]**
- **your own idea:**
  _____

3 Discuss Skills, Abilities, and Qualifications

A 🎧 **VOCABULARY. Skills and abilities. Listen and practice.**

talents abilities in art, music, mathematics, etc. that you are born with

She was born with talents in both mathematics and art.

from learn

skills abilities that you learn, such as cooking, speaking a foreign language, or driving

She has several publishing skills: writing, editing, and illustrating.

experience time spent working at a job in the past

Sally has a lot of experience in sales. She has worked at three companies.

knowledge understanding of or familiarity with a subject, gained from experience or study

Anna has extensive knowledge of the history of film. You can ask her which classics to see.

B 🎧 **LISTENING COMPREHENSION. Listen to nine people being interviewed at an international job fair. Stop after each interview and match each interviewee with his or her qualification.**

Interviewee	Qualification
_h_ **1.** Sonia Espinoza	**a.** a good memory
_d_ **2.** Silvano Lucastro	**b.** artistic ability
_f_ **3.** Ivan Martinovic *fix something with hand*	**c.** mathematical ability
_i_ **4.** Agnes Lukins	**d.** logical thinking
_e_ **5.** Elena Burgess *put myself in shoe*	**e.** compassion *, kind , nice*
_b_ **6.** Karen Trent	**f.** manual dexterity *good working with the hand*
_g_ **7.** Ed Snodgrass	**g.** common sense *figure out what todo*
_c_ **8.** Akiko Uzawa	**h.** athletic ability *sport*
_a_ **9.** Mia Kim	**i.** leadership skills

C **PAIR WORK. With your partner, classify each qualification from exercise B. Do you agree on all the classifications? Discuss your opinions.**

> ❝ I think artistic ability is a talent. You're born with it. ❞

> ❝ I disagree. I think if you study art, you can develop artistic ability. I think it's a skill. ❞

A talent	A skill
artistic ability	

STEP 1. **Take the skills inventory.**

Careers, Jobs, Advanced Studies *AND YOU*

Whether you're looking for a job or interviewing for a school,
interviewers expect you to answer questions about your interests, talents,
skills, and experience. Take this inventory to prepare yourself for those questions.

Interests
Check the fields that interest you:
- ☐ business   ☐ art
- ☐ science   ☐ manufacturing
- ☐ education   ☐ other _____

Qualifications
Check the qualifications you believe you have:
- ☐ manual dexterity   ☐ artistic ability
- ☐ logical thinking   ☐ compassion
- ☐ mathematical ability ☐ a good memory
- ☐ common sense   ☐ leadership skills
- ☐ athletic ability   ☐ other _____

Experience
Briefly note information about your experience, skills, and any special knowledge you have.

Experience: _____

Skills: _____

Special knowledge: _____

Qualification	Example
mathematical ability	I love number puzzles. I'm great at them!

STEP 2. **On the notepad, write specific examples of your qualifications.**

Qualification	Example

STEP 3. **ROLE PLAY.** **Role-play an interview for a job, for career advice, or for entry into a school. Talk about interests, qualifications, skills, and experience.**

NEED HELP? **Here's language you already know:**

Interviewer
Please tell me something about your [skills].
Do you have knowledge of [Arabic]?
What kind of [talents] do you have?
What [work] experience do you have?

Interviewee
I have experience in [teaching].
I don't have much experience.
I'm good at [math].
I have three years of [French].

4 *Discuss Work and Life Decisions*

A **READING WARM-UP.** Can you name some great humanitarians—people who have made or who are making an important difference in the world?

B 🎧 **READING.** Read about the lifework of two humanitarians. Why do you think these people are internationally known?

PEOPLE WHO CHANGED THE WORLD

Mahatma Gandhi

"Non-violence is not a weapon of the weak. It is a weapon of the strongest and the bravest." —Mahatma Gandhi

Mohandas Karamchand Gandhi believed that the way people behave is more important than what they accomplish. Gandhi studied law but became known for social action. He practiced non-violence to help India achieve independence from Britain.

In 1947, India was granted independence, but the country was broken into two states—India and Pakistan—and fighting between Hindus and Muslims began. But Gandhi believed in an India where Hindus and Muslims could live together in peace. On January 13, 1948, at the age of 78, Gandhi began a fast, not eating anything for days, with the purpose of stopping the war. After five days, the opposing leaders said they would stop the fighting and Gandhi broke his fast and started eating again.

Sadly, twelve days later Gandhi was assassinated by a Hindu fanatic who strongly opposed his vision of an India for both Hindus and Muslims. The Indian people called Gandhi "Mahatma," meaning "Great Soul."

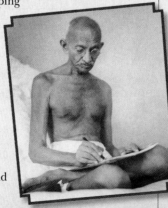

Mahatma Gandhi
Indian Spiritual / Political Leader and Humanitarian 1869–1948

Albert Schweitzer

"Man must cease attributing his problems to his environment, and learn again to exercise his will—his personal responsibility."
—Albert Schweitzer

Albert Schweitzer was born in Alsace, Germany, which is now a part of France. By the time he was 21, Schweitzer had decided on the course for his life. For nine years he would dedicate himself to the study of science, music, and religion. Then he would devote the rest of his life to serving humanity directly. Before he was 30, he was a respected writer, an organist, and an expert on the life and work of Johann Sebastian Bach.

In 1904, Schweitzer was inspired to help sick people in the world, so he studied medicine at the University of Strasbourg. He founded a hospital in French Equatorial Africa in 1913. Over the years, he built a large hospital that served thousands of Africans. In 1952, Schweitzer received the Nobel Prize for Peace. He used his $33,000 Nobel Prize to expand the hospital and to build a place to take care of people who had the terrible disease of leprosy.

Schweitzer based his personal philosophy on a love and respect for life and on a deep commitment to serve humanity through thought and action.

Albert Schweitzer
German Philosopher, Physician, and Humanitarian 1875–1965

SOURCE: Adapted from www.lucidcafe.com

C PAIR WORK. Use <u>must have</u>, <u>might have</u>, <u>may have</u>, and <u>could have</u> to discuss the following questions.

1. Why do you think Schweitzer and Gandhi spent their lives helping other people?

2. Instead of being humanitarians, what might Gandhi and Schweitzer have been? What could they have done with their lives?

D DISCUSSION. In what ways are Mahatma Gandhi and Albert Schweitzer humanitarians? Do you admire how they chose to live their lives? Do you know any other humanitarians? What did they do?

TOP NOTCH
INTERACTION • *It's never too late!*

STEP 1. On your notepad, list some plans that changed in your life. Write if you have regrets about the change.

Plans that changed	Any regrets?
I was going to be a teacher, but I changed my mind.	I have no regrets.

Plans that changed	Any regrets?

STEP 2. DISCUSSION. Discuss the plans that changed in your life. What could you have been? What might you have done? Are you sorry about it or happy about it?

NEED HELP? Here's language you already know:

Express regrets	Talk about past plans	Explain changes in plans	Express interest and offer encouragement
I could have ____ .	I was going to ____ , but ____ .	I changed my mind.	Maybe it's not too late.
I might have ____ .		My family talked me out of it.	You're still young.
I should have ____ .	I thought I would ____ , but ____ .	It's hard to make a living as a (painter).	You never know.
I wish I had ____ .		My tastes changed.	Maybe you would have hated it.

STEP 3. WRITING. Gandhi and Schweitzer had plans for their lives, but their plans changed. On a separate sheet of paper, write about your life. What were you going to do or be? What did you think you would be? Did you change your mind? What happened? Do you have any regrets? Explain.

FREE PRACTICE

A 🎧 **LISTENING COMPREHENSION.** **Listen to the conversations. Complete the chart.**

	Why did the person change his / her mind?	Any regrets?
1.		yes / no
2.		yes / no
3.		yes / no
4.		yes / no

B Complete each statement of belief about the future, using <u>would</u>.

1. When I was a child, I thought I _____.

2. My parents believed _____.

3. My teachers were sure _____.

4. When I finished school, I didn't know _____.

C Explain the meaning of each of the following qualifications. Then write an occupation or course of study for a person with each qualification.

Qualification	Definition	Occupation or Study
1. athletic ability		
2. artistic ability		
3. mathematical ability		
4. logical thinking ability		
5. a good memory		
6. leadership skills		

D Write answers to the questions about your <u>own</u> skills and qualifications.

1. What talents do you have? _____

2. What work experience do you have? _____

3. What skills do you have? _____

4. What special knowledge do you have? _____

E **WRITING.** **On a separate sheet of paper, write a paragraph about Mahatma Gandhi, Albert Schweitzer, or another great humanitarian.** Use <u>was going to</u>, <u>would</u>, <u>may</u> or <u>might have</u>, <u>must have</u>, and <u>should have</u> in your paragraph.

TOP NOTCH **PROJECT**
Write advertisements for jobs. Include requirements for experience and skills.

TOP NOTCH **WEBSITE**
For Unit 4 online activities, visit the *Top Notch* Companion Website at www.longman.com/topnotch.

UNIT WRAP-UP

- **Narration.** Tell the life story of the Wileys.
  Talk about the expectations their parents had,
  their own expectations, and what happened.

Michael	Carlota

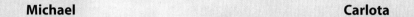

1980 — Their parents' plans and dreams for them

1990 — Their wishes and dreams for themselves

Now — Their actual choices and regrets

✓ Now I can ...

- ☐ explain a change in life and work choices.
- ☐ express regrets about decisions.
- ☐ discuss skills, abilities, and qualifications.
- ☐ discuss work and life decisions.

Holidays and Traditions

UNIT GOALS

1 Find out about a holiday
2 Ask about the customs of another culture
3 Describe a holiday or celebration
4 Explain wedding traditions

A **TOPIC PREVIEW.** Look at the pictures.
Which traditions are you familiar with?
Which ones would you like to know more about?

▲ A mariachi band in the State of Jalisco, Mexico, where mariachi was born

▲ A Korean couple dressed in the traditional hanbok

Egyptians buying traditional sweets for the feast of Eid ul-Fitr at the end of Ramadan, the most important observance in Islam ▼

▲ Thanksgiving in the United States, featuring turkey, the traditional Thanksgiving food

People in Rio de Janeiro, Brazil, enjoying Carnaval, Brazil's world-famous celebration ▼

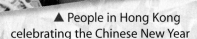

▲ People in Hong Kong celebrating the Chinese New Year

B **DISCUSSION.** Why do people think it is important to keep traditions alive? Do you think it is important to learn about the customs and traditions of other religions and cultures?

C 🎧 **SOUND BITES.** Read along silently as you listen to a conversation during a coffee break at an international meeting.

MAYA: Wow! That dress Su-min is wearing is spectacular. What was the occasion?
MIN-JIN: Chuseok. The dress is called a hanbok.
MAYA: Did you say "Chuseok"? What's that—a holiday?
MIN-JIN: That's right. It's a Korean harvest celebration. It takes place in September or October each year.

MAYA: Oh yeah? What does everybody do?
MIN-JIN: We get together with our relatives. The airports and train stations are mobbed with passengers, and the roads are impossible. It takes hours to get anywhere.
MAYA: Every country's got at least one holiday like that!

D **IN OTHER WORDS.** Say each statement in another way.

1. That dress is spectacular.

2. It takes place in September.

3. We get together with our relatives.
   spend time

4. The train stations are mobbed ~crowded~ with passengers.

5. The roads are impossible.
   a lot of traffic

E On a separate sheet of paper, write five sentences about holidays in your country. Use the following words or phrases: <u>spectacular</u>, <u>take place</u>, <u>get together with</u>, <u>mobbed with people</u>, and <u>impossible</u>.

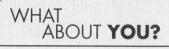

WHAT ABOUT **YOU?**

Complete the chart. Give examples and information about holiday traditions in your country.

a clothing item:	When is it worn?
a type of music:	When is it played?
a food:	When is it eaten?
a dance:	When is it danced?
a special event:	What happens?

1 ▷ Find out about a Holiday

⌂ CONVERSATION

MODEL Read and listen.

A: I heard there's going to be a holiday.

B: That's right. The Harvest Moon Festival.

A: What kind of holiday is that?

B: It's a seasonal holiday that takes place in autumn. People spend time with their families and eat moon cakes.

A: Well, have a great Harvest Moon Festival!

B: Thanks! Same to you!

⌂ **Rhythm and intonation practice**

⌂ **Types of holidays**
seasonal
historical
religious

a moon cake

 VOCABULARY.
Ways to commemorate a holiday. Listen and practice.

set off fireworks	march in parades	have picnics
pray	send cards	give each other gifts
wish each other well	remember the dead	wear costumes

B ⌂ **LISTENING COMPREHENSION.** Listen carefully to the descriptions of holidays.
Write the type of holiday and what people do to celebrate.

	Type of holiday	What people do to celebrate
Mardi Gras (U.S.)	R	wear really wild costumes, dance in huge parade
Bastille Day (France)	Historical	dance in street, eating all king food, fireworks.
Tsagaan Sar (Mongolia)	se	clean house, wear new cloth give gift

C ▸ GRAMMAR. Adjective clauses with subject relative pronouns

Use an adjective clause to identify or give information about a noun or an indefinite pronoun such as __someone__, __something__, etc. Begin an adjective clause with the relative pronouns __who__ or __that__ for adjective clauses that describe people. Use __that__ for adjective clauses that describe things.

A mariachi singer is someone **who** (or **that**) **sings traditional Mexican music**.
Carnaval is a great holiday for people **who** (or **that**) **like parades**.
Anyone **who** (or **that**) **doesn't wear a costume** can't go to the festival.
Halloween is a celebration **that takes place in October**.
The parade **that takes place on Bastille Day** is very exciting.

BE CAREFUL! Don't use a subject pronoun after the relative pronoun.
Don't say: Halloween is a celebration that ⱥ takes place in October.

GRAMMAR BOOSTER

PAGES G7–G9
For more …

D ▸ Underline the adjective clauses and circle the relative pronouns. Then draw an arrow from the relative pronoun to the noun or pronoun that it describes.

1. Ramadan is a religious tradition that is observed by Muslims all over the world.

2. Chuseok is a Korean holiday that celebrates the yearly harvest.

3. The gifts that people usually give to each other are not very expensive.

4. In the United States, a person who is invited for dinner often brings a gift to eat or drink.

5. The Day of the Dead in Mexico is a celebration that takes place in November.

6. The celebrations that take place in Brazil during Carnaval are a lot of fun.

E ▸ PAIR WORK. Create five sentences with adjective clauses to describe some holidays in your country. Use the models to begin.

| … is a (religious) holiday that … | … is a great holiday for people who … |

CONVERSATION
PAIR WORK

Role-play a conversation with a visitor to your country. Exchange information about holidays. Start like this, or create a new conversation.

A: I heard there's going to be a holiday next _____ .
B: That's right. _____ .
A: What kind of holiday is that?
B: _____ …

Continue the conversation in your own way.

> **Ways to give good wishes on holidays**
>
> Have a nice / good / great [Carnaval]!
> Have a happy [New Year]!
> Enjoy yourself on [Chuseok]!

CONTROLLED PRACTICE

2 ▶ Ask about the Customs of Another Culture

🎧 CONVERSATION MODEL Read and listen.

A: Do you mind if I ask you something?

B: Of course not. What's up?

A: I'm not sure of the customs here. When you're invited for dinner, should you bring the host a gift?

B: Yes. That's a good idea. But the gift that you bring should be small.

A: Would flowers be appropriate?

B: Absolutely perfect!

A: Thanks. It's a good thing I asked.

🎧 **Rhythm and intonation practice**

Ⓐ GRAMMAR. Adjective clauses with object relative pronouns

In some adjective clauses, the relative pronoun is the subject of the clause.
The person **who comes for dinner** should bring a gift.
[who = subject because he or she is the performer of the action]

In other adjective clauses, the relative pronoun is the object of the clause.
The person **who** [or **whom**] **you invite** should bring a gift.
[who (or whom) = object because he or she is the receiver of the action]

When the relative pronoun is the object of the clause, it may be omitted.
The book **that you bought** gives great information about holidays. OR
The book **you bought** gives great information about holidays.

When the relative pronoun is the subject of the clause, it may NOT be omitted.
The author **who wrote that book** did a great job.
NOT ~~The author wrote that book did a great job~~.

GRAMMAR BOOSTER

PAGE G9
For more …

Ⓑ 🎧 PRONUNCIATION. "Thought groups." Notice how rhythm indicates how thoughts are grouped. Listen and repeat.

1. The person who comes for dinner should bring flowers.
2. The man we invited to the party is from Senegal.
3. The song that you were listening to is fado music from Portugal.
4. The Cherry Blossom Festival is a holiday that is celebrated in Japan every spring.

maracas, traditional musical
instruments of the Caribbean
and Latin America

PAIR WORK. Discuss whether the relative pronoun can be deleted. If it can be deleted, cross it out.

1. The traditional Chinese dress ~~that~~ she has is called a cheongsam.

2. The man who you were talking with plays in a mariachi band.

3. Anzac Day is a holiday that people in Australia and New Zealand celebrate to remember the soldiers who died in wars.

4. People who visit other countries should find out about the local customs.

5. The young people whom you saw in the parade today were all wearing traditional costumes.

A bouquet of flowers is a popular gift in many countries.

 Correct the error in each sentence.

1. Putting butter on a child's nose is a birthday tradition that ~~it~~ is celebrated on the Atlantic coast of Canada.

2. On the Day of the Dead, Mexicans remember family members who they have died.

3. The older couple we saw at the restaurant they were doing the tango.

4. La Tomatina is a festival that it is celebrated in Bunol, Spain.

5. The singer performed at Casey Hall last night is well known all over Europe.

CONVERSATION PAIR WORK

Role-play a conversation with a visitor to your country. Discuss customs. Use the guide and the ideas from the box, or create a new conversation.

A: Do you mind if I ask you something?
B: Of course not. What's up?
A: I'm not sure about the customs here. When _____?
B: _____ …

Continue the conversation your <u>own</u> way.

 Some ideas…

- someone invites you out for dinner
- someone invites you to a party
- someone gives you a gift
- someone makes a special effort to help you

CONTROLLED PRACTICE

3 Describe a Holiday or Celebration

A **READING WARM-UP.** What are your favorite holiday traditions?

B 🎧 **READING.** Read about some holiday traditions and observances from around the world. Are any of them familiar to you?

HOLIDAYS AROUND THE WORLD

Thailand's Wet Water Festival

Songkran marks the start of the Buddhist New Year in Thailand. It is a wild and wonderful festival in which people of all ages have fun dousing each other with water for three solid days. If you decide to stay indoors, you'll miss out on a great time!

Songkran began nearly a thousand years ago to celebrate the beginning of the farming season. It is a time when Thai people routinely do a thorough cleaning of their homes. Additionally, people make offerings to local temples and provide food and new robes for monks.

During Songkran there is singing and dancing in the streets, and lots of water. Visitors should expect to become totally drenched—and love every minute of it! On every side street, you'll find children waiting to throw water at you. Bus riders also need to be careful. Some people have been known to hurl buckets of water through open windows!

People douse each other with water during Songkran.

Ramadan, the Month of Fasting

"May you be well throughout the year," is the typical greeting during Ramadan, the ninth month of the Islamic calendar, a special month of the year for over one billion Muslims throughout the world. According to Islamic tradition, Ramadan marks the time when Muhammad received the word of God through the Koran. Throughout the month, Muslims fast—totally abstaining from food and drinks from the break of dawn until the setting of the sun. The usual practice is to have a pre-fast meal before dawn and a post-fast meal after sunset. It is also a time of increased worship and giving to the poor and the community. Ramadan ends with the festival of Eid ul-Fitr—three days of family celebrations—and eating!

Simon Bolivar's Birthday

Simon Bolivar was born on July 24, 1783 in Caracas, Venezuela. He is known throughout Latin America as "The Liberator" because of his fight for independence from Spain. He led the armies that freed Venezuela, Bolivia, Colombia, Ecuador, Peru, and Panama. He is memorialized in many ways, but two countries celebrate his birthday every July 24th—Venezuela and Ecuador. On that day, schools and most general businesses are closed and there are military parades and government ceremonies. But the malls are open and people usually use the holiday to go shopping.

Worshippers pray during Ramadan.

Bolivar led the fight for independence from Spain.

SOURCES: www.muhajabah.com and www.colostate.edu

1. How would you categorize each of the holidays in the article—religious, seasonal, or historic?

2. Which holiday or tradition do you find the most interesting? Why?

3. Do you know any holidays, observances, or traditions that are similar to these? What are they? How are they similar and different?

TOP NOTCH
INTERACTION • *Do you mind if I ask you something?*

STEP 1. PAIR WORK. Choose three holidays in your country. Discuss them and write some notes about them on your notepad.

A historic holiday	A religious holiday	A seasonal holiday
name of holiday:	name of holiday:	name of holiday:
typical foods:	typical foods:	typical foods:
typical clothing:	typical clothing:	typical clothing:
other traditions:	other traditions:	other traditions:

STEP 2. ROLE PLAY. Take turns with a different partner. One of you is a visitor to your country. Ask about and explain your holidays and traditions. Use your notepad for ideas.

NEED HELP? **Here's language you already know:**

Resident
It's a great day for ___ .
It's customary to ___ .
It's offensive to ___ .
___ is taboo.
It's impolite to ___ .
It's probably best to ___ .
That must be ___ .
You can eat ___ .
You can wear ___ .

Visitor
Do you mind if I ask you ___?
I hear people ___ .
Is it possible to ___?
What do people do?
I'm not sure of the customs here.
Would ___ be appropriate?
It's a good thing I asked!
It's a ___ , isn't it?

traditional Japanese origami

4 Explain Wedding Traditions

A ⌒ **VOCABULARY. Getting married.** **Listen and practice.**

an engagement   an agreement to marry someone

get engaged   agree to marry

a ceremony   a formal set of actions used at an important social or religious event such as a wedding

a wedding   a marriage ceremony, especially one with a religious service

a reception   a large formal party after a ceremony

a honeymoon   a vacation taken by two newlyweds

⌒ **The wedding couple**
a bride a woman at the time she gets married
a groom a man at the time he gets married
newlyweds the bride and groom after the wedding

B Read about some wedding traditions in many English-speaking countries. Then use the vocabulary to describe a wedding tradition you are familiar with.

The bride throws her bouquet after **the wedding ceremony**. The woman who catches the bouquet is believed to be the next to get married.

The newlyweds cut the cake together **at the wedding reception**.

The groom carries the bride "across the threshold," through the doorway into their new home. Soon after the wedding, they **go on their honeymoon**.

C ⌒ **LISTENING COMPREHENSION.** **Listen carefully to Part 1 of a lecture about a traditional wedding in India. Then read the statements and listen again. Check the statements that are true. Correct the statements that are false.**

PART 1. **Before the wedding**

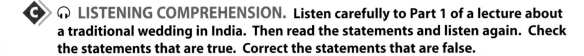

☐ **1.** A traditional Hindu wedding celebration can last for more than five days.

☐ **2.** The wedding date is chosen based on the date the bride prefers.

☐ **3.** Musicians visit the bride's home and play traditional music.

☐ **4.** The groom's relatives wash the groom with coconut or olive oil.

☐ **5.** An older person in the family offers the groom food.

☐ **6.** The bride's relatives paint her face, arms, hands, and feet.

Now listen carefully to Part 2 of the lecture. Then read the statements and listen again. Check the statements that are true. Correct the statements that are false.

PART 2. On the day of the wedding

☐ **7.** Relatives wash the bride's and groom's hands.

☐ **8.** The bride is seated behind a cloth so the groom cannot see her.

☐ **9.** Relatives throw rice grains at the bride and groom.

☐ **10.** The couple gives each other rings made of flowers and some rice.

☐ **11.** The groom places a flower necklace over the bride's neck.

D **DISCUSSION.** Are any of the traditions described in the listening similar to those in your country? Which traditions sounded the most interesting to you? Why?

TOP NOTCH
INTERACTION • *Something old and something new*

STEP 1. PAIR WORK. Read the sayings and proverbs about weddings and marriage. Explain what you think each one means. Do you find any of them offensive? What sayings or proverbs about weddings do you know in your own language?

Marry off your son when you wish. Marry off your daughter when you can.
Italy

Marriages are all happy. It's having breakfast together that causes all the trouble.
Ireland

Marriage is just friendship if there are no children.
South Africa

The woman cries before the wedding and the man after.
Poland

A bride should wear something old and something new, something borrowed, and something blue.
the U.K.

STEP 2. GROUP WORK. On your notepad, make a list of traditions for weddings in your country. Compare your lists with those of other groups.

before a wedding:

at a wedding ceremony:

STEP 3. WRITING. Write a paragraph describing the wedding traditions in your country.

after a wedding:

FREE PRACTICE

A 🎧 **LISTENING COMPREHENSION. Listen to each conversation and check the occasion or people they are talking about.**

1. ☐ the engagement ☐ the reception ☐ the honeymoon
2. ☐ the engagement ☐ the reception ☐ the honeymoon
3. ☐ the bride ☐ the groom ☐ the relatives
4. ☐ the bride ☐ the groom ☐ the relatives

B **Answer each question in your <u>own</u> way.**

1. What's the most important holiday in your country?
   What kind of a holiday is it (seasonal, historical, religious)?
   YOU _____

2. What's the longest holiday in your country? How long is it?
   YOU _____

3. What's the most interesting wedding tradition in your country?
   YOU _____

🎧 *TOP NOTCH* SONG
"Endless Holiday"
Lyrics on last page before Workbook.

TOP NOTCH PROJECT
Use the library or the Internet to research a holiday or wedding customs from another country. Tell your classmates about it.

TOP NOTCH WEBSITE
For Unit 5 online activities, visit the *Top Notch* Companion Website at www.longman.com/topnotch.

C **Complete each statement. Then write the name of a holiday or celebration for each one.**

Holiday or celebration

1. Name a holiday when people _____ fireworks. _____
2. Name a holiday when people _____ in parades. _____
3. Name a holiday when people _____ picnics. _____
4. Name a holiday when people _____ time with their families. _____
5. Name a holiday when people _____ costumes. _____
6. Name a holiday when people give _____ gifts. _____
7. Name a holiday when people wish _____ well. _____

D **Complete each sentence with an adjective clause.**

1. A groom is a man *who has just gotten married* _____.
2. Ramadan is a religious observance _____.
3. A honeymoon is a vacation _____.
4. A hanbok is a traditional dress _____.
5. Songkran is a holiday _____.
6. Simon Bolivar was a Venezuelan _____.

E **WRITING. Describe a holiday or a tradition in your country. When does it take place? What do people do? What are the origins of these customs / traditions?**

UNIT WRAP-UP

- **Vocabulary.** Name the ways people are celebrating the holiday.
- **Social language.** Create a conversation for the man and woman.
- **Grammar.** Describe what is happening on this holiday, using adjective clauses.
  There are people who are wearing costumes in the parade.

ANNUAL HOT PEPPER FESTIVAL

HOT PEPPER QUEEN!

✓ *Now I can ...*

- ☐ find out about a holiday.
- ☐ ask about the customs of another culture.
- ☐ describe a holiday or celebration.
- ☐ explain wedding traditions.

61

This is an alphabetical list of all productive vocabulary in the *Top Notch 3* units. The numbers refer to the page on which the word first appears or is defined. When a word has two meanings, both are in the list. Entries for 3A are in black. Entries for 3B are in blue.

A

abdomen 18
ability 44
absolutely 3
accept 90
acceptable 100
acupuncture 20
address (someone) 4
advice 99
advise against 99
agree 99
aloud 82
antacid 22
antibiotic 22
antihistamine 22
appointment 15
appreciate 15
appropriate 54
argue 99
arid 116
artistic ability 44
arts 38
a.s.a.p. 27
assign 34
athletic ability 44
author 76
autobiography 77
auto repair shop 31
autumn 52

B

bandage 68
battery 69
battery-operated 68
bay 110
beach 112
behavior 8
believe 102
benefit 81
bestseller 76
binding 26
biography 77
blood test 18
book on tape 82
bookshelf 79
border 110
borrow 76
bother 18
bottled water 69
bouquet 58
break (a tooth) 16
breaking news 63
breathtaking 111
bribe 104
bride 58
bridge (dental) 16
bring up 99

browse 75
budget 34
bug (n) 87
bug (v) 87
business 38
business card 26
business day 30
business school 39
button 27

C

camping trip 87
cancellation 15
canyon 116
capital city 110
capital
    punishment 102
card 52
careful 112
cashmere 32
casualty 63
catastrophic 70
caterer 34
cave 112
celebration 51
censorship 102
ceremony 58
chameleon 11
change (one's)
    mind 40
checkup 19
chest 18
chiropractic 20
chrysanthemum 12
circumstances 103
clerk 15
cliff 112
cliffhanger 76
clipping 82
coffee maker 88
coincidence 99
cold tablet 22
collect 82
come out 16
comic book 80
commemorate 52
common sense 44
compassion 44
compulsory 102
conservative 100
constitution 98
construction 70
controversial 102
conventional
    medicine 20
copy 28
copying 26

corruption 104
costume 52
cotton 32
cough 18
cough medicine 22
count on 39
courier service 30
crafts 38
criticize 80
cross-cultural
    exchange 118
crown (dental) 16
cultural heritage 118
cultural literacy 8
curl up 82
curtain 79
custom 3
custom-made 32
customary 8
cutting-edge 88

D

damage 63
danger 118
dangerous 112
dark 112
dead 52
deadly 70
death 63
death penalty 102
death toll 70
decongestant 22
decorate 34
definitely 88
deliver 28
democracy 98
dental care 14
dental emergency 16
dental school 40
dentist 15
deserve 102
destroy 66
destruction 70
develop (film) 28
developer 118
development 118
dictatorship 98
dinosaur 11
directions 90
disagree 102
disaster 62
discrimination 104
disease 39
dizzy 18
DJ 34
doable 111
document design 26

do's and don'ts 9
dosage 22
dream 39
driving age 102
drought 67
dry-clean 28
dry cleaner 30

E

earthquake 63
ecology 118
economic impact 70
ecotourism 118
education 44
efficient 30
EKG 19
election 98
emergency 15
emergency
    broadcast 68
engagement 58
enlarge 28
entirely 90
environment 118
environmental 118
environmentalist 118
environmentally
    friendly 118
epidemic 62
ethnic
    discrimination 104
etiquette 8
evacuation 68
exactly 114
examination 19
exhausting 112
experience 44
extraordinary 116
extremely 112
eye drops 22
eyewear 14

F

factory-made 32
familiar 6
family name 3
famine 67
fast read 76
fault 90
fiction 74
field (occupation) 38
filling 16
film 28
fireworks 52
first-aid kit 68
first name 3
first-name basis 3

do's and don'ts 9

first-rate 88
fit in 15
flashlight 68
flat 116
flood 67
foggy 112
forest 116
form of address 11
frame (v) 28

G

garment 32
geographic 116
get engaged 58
get into 75
get lost 90
get married 58
get together 51
gift 52
gigantic 63
government 98
groom 58
guest 15
guest list 34
guilty 80
gulf 110
gums 16

H

handle (v) 111
handmade 32
hard to follow 76
helpful 30
herbal therapy 20
high-end 88
high-tech 88
hilly 116
hip 18
hire 34
historical 52
holiday 51
homeless 62
homeopathy 20
honest 30
honeymoon 58
horrendous 87
host 54
huge 63
humanitarian 44
human rights 105
hunger 105
hurricane 67
hurry 27
hurt 16

I

immoral 80
impact 94

Social language list for 3A and 3B

This is a unit-by-unit list of the productive social language from *Top Notch 3*.

Unit 1

Allow me to introduce myself.
Everyone calls me [Surat].
Beautiful day, isn't it?
It really is.
By the way, I'm [Jane].

Do you mind my asking you the custom here?
Do you mind if I call you [Rob]?
Would it be rude to call you [Magda]?
Absolutely not.
Please do.

What would you like to be called?
How do you prefer to be addressed?
Do you use Ms. or Mrs.?
You know, you look familiar.

Unit 2

I was wondering if you might be able to recommend [a doctor].
So I hear you're from overseas.
I'm here on business.
Thanks for fitting me in.
This [tooth] is killing me.
Glad to be of help.
I really appreciate it.

Thought I'd better see someone right away.
Well, let's have a look.
I wonder if I might be able to [see the dentist].
Oh, that must hurt.
Are you in a lot of pain?

Well, let me check.
Could you be here by [3:00]?
That would be fine.
You must be [Mr. Brown].
Is anything bothering you today?
Why don't you have a seat?
I'll see if the doctor can see you.

Unit 3

You look like you're in a hurry!
I sure hope so.
But that's not all.
What else?
First thing [Monday morning]
I won't keep you, then.

Do you think I could [get this dry-cleaned by Thursday]?
That might be difficult.
I'm sorry, but it's pretty urgent.
Well, in that case, I'll see what I can do.

I have to get this to [Chicago] a.s.a.p.
Can you recommend a [courier service]?
Why don't you have [Aero Flash] take care of it?
They're really reliable.

Unit 4

I wish I'd [gone to medical school].
Since when have you been [interested in medicine]?
I could have [made a difference].
Maybe it's not too late.
Think so?
Sorry about that.
You can count on me.
Long time no see.
How have you been?

Not bad, thanks.
So what are you doing these days?
No kidding!
How come?
It's hard to make a living [as a painter].
My tastes changed.
My family talked me out of it.
I just changed my mind.
Why do you think that?
Could be. But you never know.

Please tell me something about your [skills].
Do you have knowledge of [Arabic]?
What kind of [talents] do you have?
What [work] experience do you have?
I have experience in [teaching].
I don't have much experience.
I'm good at [math].
I have three years of [French].

Unit 5

[That dress is] spectacular!
What was the occasion?
It takes place [in September].
Oh yeah?
We get together with our [relatives].
[The roads are] impossible.
It takes hours to get anywhere.

I heard there's going to be [a holiday].
What kind of [holiday] is that?
People spend time with their [families].
Have a great [holiday]!
Same to you!
Do you mind if I ask you something?

Of course not.
What's up?
I'm not sure of [the customs here].
Would [flowers] be appropriate?
Absolutely perfect!
It's a good thing I asked.

Unit 6

Oh, my goodness!
What happened?
What a disaster!
That's gigantic!
Any word on [casualties]?
Let's hope for the best.

I wonder if [8.6 is a record].
Believe it or not.
I'm on the line with [your parents].
Would you like to say hello?
I'm running late.
Anything you'd like me to tell them?

There's a storm on its way.
Will do.
What's going on [in the news today]?
What a shame.
Thank goodness [for that].

Unit 7

Looking for anything special?
I'm just browsing.
What are you up to?
I'm picking up [some gardening magazines].
She can't get enough of [them].
Are you reading anything good these days?
Not really.
I just can't seem to get into it.

I guess [poetry] just doesn't turn me on.
I can't put it down.
It's a real page-turner.
Thanks for the tip.
Don't bother.
What's that you're reading?
I've always wanted to read that!
Is it any good?
It's hard to follow.
It's a fast read.

I'd highly recommend it.
Do you mind if I borrow it when you're done?
Not at all.
What incredible [bread]!
I learned how [in the latest issue of Home magazine].
I didn't know they had [recipes].
I'm all thumbs!

Unit 8

[The bugs were] horrendous.
I got eaten alive.
Don't you wish someone would [invent something that works]?
Where have you been?
No way!
I don't believe it.

Do you think I should get the [Brew Rite]?
It's on sale.
That depends.
How much are they selling it for?
Definitely.
That's a great price.
It's top of the line.

Sorry we're late.
We got lost.
That's OK.
It can happen to anyone.
It was entirely my fault.
Better late than never.
Let me get you something to [drink].

Unit 9

So what are you up to these days?
What a coincidence.
I've been meaning to [give you a call].
Would it be rude to [bring that up at the dinner table]?
It would not be cool to [argue with them].
How well you know me!
I do tend to be [a little opinionated].
In general, is it acceptable here to [ask people about politics]?
Would it be OK to [ask you]?

What would you like to know?
That's a good question!
Are you in favor of [capital punishment]?
What about you?
Actually, I'm against [the death penalty].
I think it's wrong to [take a life], no matter what.
I'm opposed to [censorship].
I guess we'll have to agree to disagree.
I have to disagree with you there.
I'm not sure I agree.
I'm afraid I don't agree.

I agree with you on that one.
I couldn't agree more.
I couldn't have said it better myself.
That's exactly what I think.
It's OK, under some circumstances.
That may be true, but ___.
I see what you mean, but ___.
Well, on one hand ___. But on the other hand, ___.
That's one way to look at it.

Unit 10

You wouldn't happen to know anything about [La Fortuna], would you?
Is it worth seeing?
You definitely don't want to miss it.
The whole setting is really [breathtaking].
I can't wait.
Watch out on the way down.
Be sure to take it slow.

Thanks for the warning.
Do you think that's all doable in [two days]?
I'm sure you could handle both.
Can you tell me the way to [the beach].
That way.
Not at all.
[The undertow] can be quite [dangerous].

Where exactly is [Miyajima] located?
About [an hour west of Osaka by train].
Are you planning on going?
I've been thinking about it.
It's a must see.
Be sure to [take pictures]!
You don't want to miss it.
It's overrated.
It's a waste of time.

Pronunciation table

These are the pronunciation symbols used in *Top Notch 3*.

Vowels

symbol	key word	symbol	key word
i	beat, feed	ə	banana, among
ɪ	bit, did	ɚ	shirt, murder
eɪ	date, paid	aɪ	bite, cry, buy, eye
ɛ	bet, bed	aʊ	about, how
æ	bat, bad	ɔɪ	voice, boy
ɑ	box, odd, father	ɪr	deer
ɔ	bought, dog	ɛr	bare
oʊ	boat, road	ɑr	bar
ʊ	book, good	ɔr	door
u	boot, food, flu	ʊr	tour
ʌ	but, mud, mother		

Consonants

symbol	key word	symbol	key word
p	pack, happy	z	zip, please, goes
b	back, rubber	ʃ	ship, machine, station, special, discussion
t	tie		
d	die		
k	came, key, quick	ʒ	measure, vision
g	game, guest	h	hot, who
tʃ	church, nature, watch	m	men
dʒ	judge, general, major	n	sun, know, pneumonia
f	fan, photograph	ŋ	sung, ringing
v	van	w	wet, white
θ	thing, breath	l	light, long
ð	then, breathe	r	right, wrong
s	sip, city, psychology	y	yes
		t̬	butter, bottle
		t̚	button

Irregular verbs

base form	simple past	past participle	base form	simple past	past participle
be	was / were	been	lend	lent	lent
become	became	become	let	let	let
begin	began	begun	lose	lost	lost
bite	bit	bit / bitten	make	made	made
bleed	bled	bled	mean	meant	meant
break	broke	broken	meet	met	met
bring	brought	brought	pay	paid	paid
build	built	built	put	put	put
burn	burned / burnt	burned / burnt	quit	quit	quit
buy	bought	bought	read /rid/	read /rɛd/	read /rɛd/
catch	caught	caught	ride	rode	ridden
choose	chose	chosen	ring	rang	rung
come	came	come	rise	rose	risen
cost	cost	cost	run	ran	run
cut	cut	cut	say	said	said
do	did	done	see	saw	seen
draw	drew	drawn	sell	sold	sold
dream	dreamed / dreamt	dreamed / dreamt	send	sent	sent
drink	drank	drunk	sew	sewed	sewn
drive	drove	driven	shake	shook	shaken
eat	ate	eaten	sing	sang	sung
fall	fell	fallen	sit	sat	sat
feed	fed	fed	sleep	slept	slept
feel	felt	felt	speak	spoke	spoken
fight	fought	fought	spend	spent	spent
find	found	found	spread	spread	spread
fit	fit	fit	stand	stood	stood
flee	fled	fled	steal	stole	stolen
fly	flew	flown	stuck	stuck	stuck
forbid	forbade / forbid	forbidden	sting	stung	stung
forget	forgot	forgotten	strike	struck	struck
get	got	gotten	swim	swam	swum
give	gave	given	take	took	taken
go	went	gone	teach	taught	taught
grow	grew	grown	tell	told	told
have	had	had	think	thought	thought
hear	heard	heard	throw	threw	thrown
hit	hit	hit	understand	understood	understood
hold	held	held	wake up	woke up	woken up
hurt	hurt	hurt	wear	wore	worn
keep	kept	kept	win	won	won
know	knew	known	write	wrote	written
leave	left	left			

Verb tense review: present, past, and future

 ## THE PRESENT OF <u>BE</u>

Statements

I	am	
You We They	are	late.
He She It	is	

 ## THE SIMPLE PRESENT TENSE

Statements

I You We They	speak English.
He She	speaks English.

<u>Yes</u> / <u>no</u> questions

Do	I you we they	know them?
Does	he she	eat meat?

Short answers

Yes,	I you we they	do.
	he she it	does.

No,	I you we they	don't.
	he she it	doesn't.

Information questions

What do	you we they	need?
When does	he she it	start?
Who	wants needs likes	this book?

 ## THE PRESENT CONTINUOUS

Statements

I	am	watching TV.
You We They	are	studying English.
He She It	is	arriving now.

<u>Yes</u> / <u>no</u> questions

Am	I	
Are	you we they	going too fast?
Is	he she it	

Short answers

Yes,	I	am.
	you	are.
	he she it	is.
	we they	are.

No,	I'm not.
	you aren't / you're not.
	he isn't / he's not.
	she isn't / she's not.
	it isn't / it's not.
	we aren't / we're not.
	they aren't / they're not.

Information questions

What	are	you we they	doing?
When	is	he she it	leaving?
Where	am	I	staying tonight?
Who	is		driving?

 ## THE PAST CONTINUOUS

Statements

I	was	singing that song.
You We They	were	playing the piano.
He She It	was	leaving from Central Station.

<u>Yes</u> / <u>no</u> questions

Was	I he she it	
Were	we you they	landing in Sydney when the storm began?

Short answers

Yes,	I he she it	was.
	we you they	were.

No,	I he she it	wasn't.
	we you they	weren't.

Information questions

When	was	I / he / she / it	speeding?
Where	were	we / you / they	going?
Who	was		arriving?

5 THE PAST OF BE

Statements

I / He / She / It	was late.
We / You / They	were early.

Yes / no questions

Was	I / he / she / it	on time?
Were	we / you / they	in the same class?

Short answers

Yes,	I / he / she / it	was.
	we / you / they	were.

No,	I / he / she / it	wasn't.
	we / you / they	weren't.

Information questions

Where	were	we? / you? / they?	
When	was	he / she / it	here?
Who	were	they?	
Who	was	he? / she? / it?	

6 THE SIMPLE PAST TENSE

Many verbs are irregular in the simple past tense.
See the list of irregular verbs on page A5.

Statements

I / You / He / She / It / We / They	stopped working.

I / You / He / She / It / We / They	didn't start again.

Yes / no questions

Did	I / you / he / she / it / we / they	make a good dinner?

Short answers

Yes,	I / you / he / she / it / we / they	did.

No,	I / you / he / she / it / we / they	didn't.

Information questions

When did	I / you / he / she / it / we / they	read that?
Who		called?

7 THE FUTURE WITH WILL

Affirmative and negative statements

I / You / He / She / It / We / They	will / won't	stop at five o'clock.

Yes / no questions

Will	I / you / he / she / it / we / they	be on time?

Affirmative and negative short answers

Yes,	I you he	will.
No,	she it we they	won't.

Information questions

What will	I you he she it we they	do?
Who will		be there?

THE FUTURE WITH <u>BE GOING TO</u>

Statements

I'm You're He's She's It's We're They're	going to	be here soon.

I'm You're He's She's It's We're They're	not going to	be here soon.

<u>Yes</u> / <u>no</u> questions

Are	you we they	going to want coffee?
Am	I	going to be late?
Is	he she it	going to arrive on time?

Short answers

Yes,	I	am.
	you	are.
	he she it	is.
	we they	are.

No,	I'm not. you aren't / you're not. he isn't / he's not. she isn't / she's not. it isn't / it's not. we aren't / we're not. they aren't / they're not.

Information questions

What	are	you / we / they	going to see?
When	is	he / she / it	going to shop?
Where	am	I	going to stay tomorrow?
Who	is		going to call?

THE PRESENT PERFECT

Affirmative and negative statements

I You We They	have haven't	left yet.
He She It	has hasn't	

<u>Yes</u> / <u>no</u> questions

Have	I you we they	said enough?
Has	he she it	already started?

Affirmative and negative short answers

Yes, No,	I you we they	have. haven't.
Yes, No,	he she it	has. hasn't.

Information questions

Where	have	I you we they	seen that book?
How	has	he she it	been?
Who	has		read it?

THE PASSIVE VOICE

Form the passive voice with a form of <u>be</u> and the past participle of the verb		
	ACTIVE VOICE	**PASSIVE VOICE**
simple present	Art collectors **buy** famous paintings.	Famous paintings **are bought by** art collectors.
present continuous	The Cineplex **is showing** that film.	That film **is being shown** by the Cineplex.
present perfect	All the critics **have reviewed** that book.	That book **has been reviewed** by all the critics.
simple past	Vera Wang **designed** this dress.	This dress **was designed** by Vera Wang.
past continuous	Last year, World Air **was** still **selling** tours to the Ivory Coast.	Last year, tours to the Ivory coast **were** still **being sold.**
future with <u>will</u>	The children **will return** the books tomorrow.	The books **will be returned** tomorrow.
<u>be going to</u>	Bart's Garage **is going to repair** my car this afternoon.	My car is **going to be repaired** by Bart's Garage this afternoon.

Verbs followed by a gerund

acknowledge	delay	escape	keep	prohibit	resent
admit	deny	explain	mention	propose	resist
advise	detest	feel like	mind	quit	risk
appreciate	discontinue	finish	miss	recall	suggest
avoid	discuss	forgive	postpone	recommend	support
can't help	dislike	give up	practice	regret	tolerate
celebrate	endure	imagine	prevent	report	understand
consider	enjoy	justify			

Verbs followed directly by an infinitive

afford	choose	help	mean	pretend	volunteer
agree	consent	hesitate	need	promise	wait
appear	decide	hope	neglect	refuse	want
arrange	deserve	hurry	offer	request	wish
ask	expect	intend	pay	seem	would like
attempt	fail	learn	plan	struggle	yearn
can't wait	grow	manage	prepare	swear	

Verbs followed by an object before an infinitive*

advise	convince	get	order	remind	urge
allow	enable	help	pay	request	want
ask	encourage	hire	permit	require	warn
cause	expect	invite	persuade	teach	wish
challenge	forbid	need	promise*	tell	would like
choose	force				

* These verbs can also be followed by the infinitive without an object (example: *want to speak* or *want someone to speak*).

Verbs followed by either a gerund or an infinitive

begin	hate	remember*
can't stand	like	start
continue	love	stop*
forget*	prefer	try

* There is a big difference in meaning when these verbs are followed by a gerund or an infinitive.

Adjectives followed by an infinitive*

afraid	curious	disturbed	fortunate	pleased	shocked
alarmed	delighted	eager	glad	proud	sorry
amazed	depressed	easy	happy	ready	surprised
angry	determined	embarrassed	hesitant	relieved	touched
anxious	disappointed	encouraged	likely	reluctant	upset
ashamed	distressed	excited	lucky	sad	willing

* EXAMPLE: I'm willing to accept that.

3A

GRAMMAR BOOSTER

The *Grammar Booster* is optional. It provides more explanation and practice, as well as additional grammar concepts.

UNIT 1   Lesson 1

A   Correct the error in each item.

1. They'd both like to study abroad, would they?
2. It's only a six-month course, is it?
3. Clark met his wife on a rafting trip, didn't Clark?
4. Marian made three trips to Japan last year, hasn't she?
5. There were a lot of English-speaking people on the tour, wasn't it?
6. The students don't know anything about that, don't they?
7. There isn't any problem with my student visa, isn't there?
8. It's always interesting to travel with people from other countries, aren't they?
9. With English, you can travel to most parts of the world, can you?
10. I'm next, are I?

UNIT 1   Lesson 2

┌─ **Review: verb usage in the present and past** ──────────

The simple present tense (and NOT the present continuous)

for facts and regular occurrences
I **study** English. Class **meets** every day. Water **boils** at 100°.

with frequency adverbs and time expressions
They never **eat** before 6:00 on weekdays.

with stative (non-action) verbs
I **remember** her now.

for future actions, especially those indicating schedules
Flight 100 usually **leaves** at 2:00, but tomorrow it leaves at 1:30.

The present continuous (and NOT the simple present tense)

for actions happening now (but NOT with stative verbs)
They**'re talking** on the phone.

for actions occurring during a time period in the present
This year I**'m studying** English.

for some future actions, especially those already planned
Thursday I**'m going** to the theater.

The present perfect or the present perfect continuous

for unfinished or continuous actions
I**'ve lived** here since 2001. OR I**'ve been living** here since 2001.
I**'ve lived** here for five years. OR I**'ve been living** here for five years.

Stative (non-action) verbs

appear	have	own	suppose
be	hear	possess	taste
believe	know	prefer	think
belong	like	remember	understand
contain	look	see	want
cost	love	seem	weigh
feel	need	smell	
hate	notice	sound	

Review: verb usage in the present and past (continued)

The present perfect (but NOT the present perfect continuous)

for completed or non-continuing actions

I've **eaten** there three times.

I've never **read** that book.

I've already **seen** him.

The simple past tense

for actions completed at a specified time in the past

I **ate** there in 2003. NOT ~~I've eaten~~ there in 2003.

The past continuous

for one or more actions in progress at a time in the past

At 7:00, we **were eating** dinner.

They **were swimming** and we **were sitting** on the beach.

The past continuous and the simple past

for an action that interrrupted a continuing action in the past

I **was eating** when my sister **called**.

Used to

for past situations and habits that no longer exist

I **used to smoke**, but I stopped.

They **didn't use to require** a visa, but now they do.

The past perfect

to indicate that one past action preceded another past action

When I arrived, they **had finished** lunch.

A **Correct the verbs in the following sentences.**

1. I talk on the phone with my fiancé right now.
2. She's usually avoiding sweets.
3. They eat dinner now and can't talk on the phone.
4. Every Friday I'm going to the gym at 7:00.
5. Burt is wanting to go home early.
6. This year we all study English.
7. The train is never leaving before 8:00.
8. Water is freezing when the temperature goes down.
9. We're liking coffee.
10. On most days I'm staying home.

B **Complete each sentence with the present perfect continuous.**

1. We _____ to this spa for two years.
   come
2. *Lost in Translation* _____ at the Classic Cinema since last Saturday.
   play
3. Robert _____ for an admissions letter from the language school for a week.
   wait
4. The tour operators _____ weather conditions for the rafting trip.
   worry about
5. I _____ that tour with everyone.
   talk about

C Check the sentences and questions that express unfinished or continuing actions. Change the verb phrase in those sentences to the present perfect continuous.

☐ **1.** The Averys have lived in New York since the late nineties.

☐ **2.** Their relatives have already called them.

☐ **3.** We have waited to see them for six months.

☐ **4.** I haven't seen the Berlin Philharmonic yet.

☐ **5.** This is the first time I've visited Dubai.

☐ **6.** We have eaten in that old Peruvian restaurant for years.

☐ **7.** Has he ever met your father?

☐ **8.** How long have they studied Arabic?

☐ **9.** My husband still hasn't bought a car.

☐ **10.** The kids have just come back from the race.

D Complete each sentence using the past continuous in one blank and the simple past tense in the other.

1. I _____ when I _____ the accident.
              speed   have

2. They _____ TV when they _____ the news.
             watch   hear

3. What _____ when I _____?
          you / do   call

4. People _____ for the theater to open when the fire _____.
           wait   start

5. Who _____ the computer when the electricity _____ off?
        use   go

UNIT 2   *Lesson 1*

┌─ **May, might,** and **must:** degrees of certainty ─────────────────

He's carrying a violin.   certainty (a fact)

He **must** be a musician.   probability (probably true)

He **might (may)** play very well.   possibility (could be true)

A Write a statement of certainty, possibility, and probability about the person in each picture.

1.   certainty   <u>He's in a lot of pain.</u>

        possibility   _____

        probability   _____

2.   certainty   _____

        possibility   _____

        probability   _____

3.   certainty   _____

        possibility   _____

        probability   _____

UNIT 3 Lesson 1

The passive causative: the <u>by</u> phrase

Use a <u>by</u> phrase if knowing who performed the action is important.

I had my shoes repaired **by a young man** at the train station.

If knowing who performed the action is <u>not</u> important, you don't need to include a <u>by</u> phrase.

I had my shoes repaired ~~by someone~~ at the train station.

A **Use the cues to write advice about services with the passive causative.**

1. shoe / repair / Mr. Gil / Boot Stop *Get your shoes repaired by Mr. Gil at the Boot Stop.*

2. picture / framed / Lydia / Austin Custom Framing _____

3. hair / cut / Eva / Bella Gente Hair Salon _____

4. photos / process / mall _____

5. custom suit / make / Luigi _____

6. dry cleaning / do/ Midtown Dry Cleaners _____

UNIT 3 Lesson 2

A **Complete each sentence with an infinitive, a base form, or a past participle.**

1. They got the dry cleaner _____ the suit again.
_{clean}

2. He had the photographer _____ pictures of everyone in the family.
_{take}

3. I missed class, so I got my classmates _____ me what happened that day
in class.
_{tell}

4. Are you going to have those pants _____?
_{shorten}

5. She made her son _____ in bed because he wasn't feeling well.
_{stay}

6. I'd better get to the bank before it closes if I want to get that check _____.
_{cash}

7. Our teacher had us _____ about what we did during the vacation.
_{write}

8. You'd better get the travel agent _____ your flight right away.
_{change}

9. Are you going to get your paintings _____ for the art exhibit?
_{frame}

10. If you need to know when the next train leaves, you can have my assistant _____
the station.
_{call}

<u>Let</u>

Use <u>let</u> to show that someone permits someone to do something.

I **don't let** my children **stay** out after 9:00.   Why don't you **let** me **help** you?

<u>Let</u> is followed by an object and the base form of a verb.

	object	base form	
She **let**	her sister	**wear**	her skirt.

NOT She let her sister ~~to wear~~ her skirt.

On a separate sheet of paper, rewrite each sentence using <u>let</u>.

1. Don't permit your little brother to open the oven door.
2. You should permit your little sister to go to the store with you.
3. Actually, we don't permit our daughter to eat a lot of candy.
4. I wouldn't permit my youngest son to go to the mall alone.
5. Why won't you permit him to see that movie?
6. You should permit the tailor to do what he thinks is best.
7. We always permit him to stay out late.

Causative <u>have</u> and the past perfect auxiliary <u>have</u>

BE CAREFUL! Don't confuse the simple past tense causative <u>have</u> with <u>have</u> used in the past perfect.

I <u>had them call</u> me before 10:00.   (They called me.)
I <u>had called</u> them before 10:00.   (I called them.)

 Who did what? Read the sentence. Complete the statement.

1. We had them fix the car before our trip.   <u>They</u> fixed <u>the car</u>.
   We had fixed the car before our trip.   _____ fixed _____.

2. Janet had already called her mother.   _____ called _____.
   Janet had her mother call the train station.   _____ called _____.

3. Mark had his classmate help him with it.   _____ helped _____.
   Mark had helped his classmate with it.   _____ helped _____.

4. My father had signed the check for his boss.   _____ signed _____.
   My father had his boss sign the check.   _____ signed _____.

5. Mr. Gates had them open the bank early.   _____ opened _____.
   Mr. Gates had opened the bank early.   _____ opened _____.

UNIT 4   Lesson 1

REVIEW: Expressing the future

The future can be expressed in all the following ways:

<u>will</u> + base form	I'll see	
<u>be going to</u> + base form	I'm going to see	her tomorrow.
the simple present tense	I see	
the present continuous	I'm seeing	

Modals can also be used to talk about the future.

	I might see	
modal + base form	I may see	her tomorrow.
	I can see	

REVIEW: Future with will and be going to

Use **will** or **be going to** to make a prediction or to say that something in the future
will be true. There is no difference in meaning.

Getting a new car **will cost** a lot of money.   Getting a new car **is going to cost** a lot of money.

Use **be going to** to express a plan.

My tooth has been killing me all week. I'm **going to call** a dentist.   NOT ~~I will call~~ a dentist.

Use **will** for willingness.

A: Is it true you won't go to the dentist?

B: I'**ll go** to the dentist, but I don't like fillings.   NOT ~~I'm going to go~~…

A **Complete the conversations using will or be going to.**

1. A: Would you like to go running in the park? I _____ in about half an hour.
_{leave}

B: That sounds great. I _____ you there.
_{meet}

2. A: It's midnight. Why are you still reading?

B: We _____ a test tomorrow.
_{have}

3. A: Do you have plans for tomorrow?

B: Yes. I _____ a chiropractor for the first time.
_{see}

4. A: I hope you can come tomorrow night. We'd really like you to be there.

B: OK. I _____ .
_{come}

5. A: I'm thinking about getting a new laptop.

B: Really? Well, I _____ you mine. I love it.
_{show}

**REVIEW: The present continuous, the simple present tense,
and modals with future meaning**

The present continuous

My tooth has been killing me all week. I'**m calling** the dentist tomorrow.

What **are** you **doing** this afternoon? I'**m going** to the beach.

The simple present tense

The office is usually open until 9:00, but it **closes** at 6:00 tomorrow.

Modals should, could, ought to, may, might, have to, and can

You **could** catch the next bus. We **should** call her next week.

B **Read each sentence. Check the sentences that have future meaning.**

☐ **1.** Hannah is studying English this month.

☐ **2.** Max is studying French next month.

☐ **3.** Nancy studies English in the evening.

☐ **4.** I'm taking my daughter out for dinner tonight.

☐ **5.** You should call me tomorrow.

☐ **6.** He might have time to see you later.

☐ **7.** My parents are arriving at 10:00.

☐ **8.** The class finishes at 3:00 today.

☐ **9.** The class always starts at 2:00 and finishes at 4:00.

☐ **10.** We may stay another week in Paris.

UNIT 4   Lesson 2

> **Regrets about the past: <u>wish</u> + the past perfect; <u>should have</u> and <u>ought to have</u>**
>
> **<u>wish</u> + the past perfect**
>
> **You can express a regret about the past with <u>wish</u> + the past perfect.**
>
> I **wish** I **had married** later. And I **wish** I **hadn't married** Celine!
>
> Do you **wish** you **had bought** that car when it was available?
>
> **<u>should have</u> and <u>ought to have</u>**
>
> **<u>Ought to have</u> has the same meaning as <u>should have</u>. <u>Should have</u> is much more common in spoken English.**
>
> I **should have married** later. = I **ought to have married** later.
>
> I **shouldn't have married** Celine. = I **ought not to have** married Celine.
>
> **Should** he **have married** Celine? = **Ought** he **to have** married Celine?
>
> **Note: American English speakers use <u>should have</u> instead of <u>ought to have</u> in negative statements and in questions.**

A **Restate the statements and questions with <u>wish</u> + the past perfect to statements and questions with <u>should have</u> or <u>ought to have</u>.**

1. I wish I had studied law. (should) *I should have studied law.*

2. She wishes she had had children. (ought to) _____

3. Do you wish you had studied Chinese? (should) _____

4. I wish I had gone to Chile instead of Australia. (ought to) _____

5. Do you wish you had taken the job at the embassy? (should) _____

UNIT 5   Lesson 1

A **On a separate sheet of paper, combine the two sentences into one sentence, making the second sentence an adjective clause. Use <u>who</u> or <u>that</u>.**

1. The hotel clerk was very helpful. / He recommended the restaurant.

   The hotel clerk who recommended the restaurant was very helpful.

2. My cousin called today. / He lives in New Zealand.

3. We have a meeting every morning. / It begins at 9:30.

4. The celebration is spectacular. / It takes place in spring.

5. The teacher is not very formal. / She teaches the grammar class.

6. Patients might prefer homeopathy. / They want to avoid strong medication.

7. The copy shop is closed on weekends. / It offers express service.

8. The hotel is very expensive. / It has a swimming pool.

9. Do you like the teacher? / He teaches the grammar class.

Reciprocal pronouns: <u>each other</u> and <u>one another</u>

<u>Each other</u> and <u>one another</u> have the same meaning, but <u>one another</u> is more formal.

   People give **each other** (or **one another**) gifts.   Friends send **each other** (or **one another**) cards.

BE CAREFUL! Reciprocal pronouns have a different meaning from reflexive pronouns.

   They looked at **themselves**. (Each person looked in a mirror.)

   They looked at **each other**. (Each person looked at the other person.)

B **On a separate sheet of paper, rewrite each underlined phrase using a reciprocal pronoun.**

   1. On Christmas, in many places in the world, people <u>give and receive presents</u>.

   On Christmas, in many places in the world, people give each other presents.

   2. On New Year's Eve in New York City, people wait in Times Square for midnight to come so they can <u>kiss other people</u> and <u>wish other people</u> a happy new year.

   3. During the Thai holiday Songkran, people <u>throw water at other people</u> on the street.

   4. During the Tomato Festival in Bunol, Spain, people have a lot of fun <u>throwing tomatoes at other people</u> for about two hours.

   5. After a day of fasting during Ramadan, Muslims around the world <u>invite other people to eat</u> in their homes in the evening.

Reflexive pronouns

A reflexive pronoun should always agree with the subject of the verb.

   People really enjoy **themselves** during Carnaval.

   My sister made **herself** sick from eating so much!

Common expressions with reflexive pronouns

believe in oneself	If you **believe in yourself**, you can do anything.
enjoy oneself	We **enjoyed ourselves** very much on our vacation.
feel sorry for oneself	Don't sit around **feeling sorry for yourself**.
help oneself to (something)	Please **help yourselves** to dessert!
hurt oneself	Paul **hurt himself** when he tried to move the refrigerator.
give oneself (something)	I wanted to **give myself** a gift, so I bought a watch.
introduce oneself	Why don't you **introduce yourself** to your new neighbor?
be proud of oneself	Jackie was really **proud of herself** when she got that job.
take care of oneself	You should **take** better **care of yourself**. OK?
talk to oneself	I sometimes **talk to myself** when I'm feeling nervous.
teach oneself (to do something)	Niki **taught herself** to use a computer.
tell oneself (something)	I always **tell myself** I'm not going to eat dessert, and then I do anyway.
work for oneself	Oscar left the company last year. He now **works for himself**.

Reflexive pronouns

me	→	myself
you	→	yourself
him	→	himself
her	→	herself
it	→	itself
us	→	ourselves
them	→	themselves

C **Complete the sentences with reflexive pronouns.**

   1. My brother and his wife really enjoyed _____ on their vacation.

   2. My uncle has been teaching _____ how to cook.

   3. The food was so terrific that I helped _____ to some more!

   4. Don't sit around feeling sorry for _____.

   5. I hope your sister's been taking good care of _____.

   6. I didn't know anyone at the party, and I was too shy to introduce _____ to anyone.

   7. Mr. Yu hurt _____ while lighting firecrackers for the Chinese New Year.

D Complete each sentence with one of the common expressions with reflexive pronouns.

1. When did your brother _____ how to play the guitar?

2. You'd better tell your daughter to stop playing near that stove or she'll _____.

3. I really hope you _____ when you're on vacation!

4. To practice greetings and introductions, I ask my students to _____ to each other on the first day of class.

---
by + reflexive pronouns

Use by with a reflexive pronoun to mean "alone."

> You cannot put on a kimono **by yourself**. You need help.
> Students cannot learn to speak in English **by themselves**. They need to practice with each other.

E Complete each sentence with **by** and a reflexive pronoun.

1. Very young children shouldn't be allowed to play outside _____.

2. Did your father go to the store _____?

3. When did you learn to fix a computer _____?

4. We got tired of waiting, so we found a table _____.

UNIT 5 Lesson 2

Adjective clauses: who and whom in formal English

In formal written or spoken English, use who for subject relative pronouns and whom for object relative pronouns.

> The singer was terrible. + **He** sang in the restaurant.
>   subject relative pronoun
> The singer **who** sang in the restaurant was terrible.

> The singer was terrible. + We heard **him** last night.
>   object relative pronoun
> The singer **whom** we heard last night was terrible.

A Complete the sentences with **who** or **whom**.

1. The manager _____ works at that hotel is very helpful.

2. The man _____ I met at the meeting has invited us to lunch.

3. The sales representative _____ lives in Hong Kong may apply for that job.

4. I am very satisfied with the hair stylist _____ you recommended.

5. The guests _____ we invited to the event were three hours late.

6. The dentist _____ you'll see tomorrow speaks English.

7. The DJ _____ you requested is performing at the club tonight.

8. The tailor _____ I'm recommending is very reasonable.

9. My friend _____ works at the embassy will help you.

10. Is your colleague someone _____ I can really trust?

🎵 TOP NOTCH POP LYRICS FOR 3A AND 3B

It's a Great Day for Love [Unit 1]

Wherever you go,
there are things you should know,
so be aware
of the customs and views—
all the do's and taboos—
of people there.
You were just a stranger in a sea of new
faces.
Now we're making small talk on a
first-name basis.
(CHORUS)
It's a great day for love, isn't it?
Aren't you the one I was hoping to find?
It's a great day for love, isn't it?
By the time you said hello,
I had already made up my mind.
Wherever you stay
be sure to obey
the golden rules,
and before you relax,
brush up on the facts
you learned at school.
Try to be polite and always be sure to get
some friendly advice on proper etiquette.
(CHORUS)
and when you smiled at me
and I fell in love,
the sun had just appeared
in the sky above.
You know how much I care, don't you?
And you'll always be there, won't you?
(CHORUS)

I'll Get Back to You [Unit 3]

Your camera isn't working right.
It needs a few repairs.
You make me ship it overnight.
Nothing else compares.
You had to lengthen your new skirt,
and now you want to get
someone to wash your fancy shirts
and dry them when they're wet.
Come a little closer—
let me whisper in your ear.
Is my message getting across
to you loud and clear?
(CHORUS)
You're always making plans.
I'll tell you what I'll do:
let me think it over and
I'll get back to you.
You want to get your suit dry-cleaned.
You want to get someone
to shorten your new pair of jeans
and call you when they're done.
I guess I'll have them print a sign
and hang it on your shelf,
with four small words in one big line:
"Just do it yourself."
Let me tell you what this song
is really all about.
I'm getting tired of waiting while you
figure it out.
I've heard all your demands,

but I have a life too.
Let me think it over and
I'll get back to you.
I'm really reliable,
incredibly fast,
extremely helpful
from first to last.
Let me see what I can do.
Day after day,
everybody knows
I always do what I say.
(CHORUS)

Endless Holiday [Unit 5]

Day after day,
all my thoughts drift away
before they've begun.
I sit in my room
in the darkness and gloom
just waiting for someone
to take me to a tourist town,
with parties in the street and people
dancing to a joyful sound.
(CHORUS)
It's a song that people sing.
It's the laughter that you bring
on an endless holiday.
It's the happiness inside.
It's a roller coaster ride
on an endless holiday.
I try and I try
to work hard, but I
get lost in a daze,
and I think about
how sad life is without
a few good holidays.
I close my eyes, pull down the shade,
and in my imagination I am dancing in a
big parade,
and the music is loud.
I get lost in the crowd
on an endless holiday.
It's a picnic at noon.
It's a trip to the moon
on an endless holiday,
with flags and confetti,
wild costumes and a great big marching
band,
as we wish each other well
in a language we all understand.
The sky above fills with the light
of fireworks exploding, as we dance along
the street tonight.
(CHORUS)

Lucky to Be Alive [Unit 6]
(CHORUS)
Thank you for helping me to survive.
I'm really lucky to be alive.
When I was caught in a freezing
snowstorm,
you taught me how to stay warm.
When I was running from a landslide
with no place to hide,
you protected me from injury.
Even the world's biggest tsunami

has got nothing on me,
because you can go faster.
You keep me safe from disaster.
You're like some kind of hero—
you're the best friend that I know.
(CHORUS)
When the big flood came with
the pouring rain,
they were saying that a natural
disaster loomed.
You just opened your umbrella.
You were the only fellow who kept calm
and prepared.
You found us shelter.
I never felt like anybody cared
the way that you did when you said,
"I will always be there—
you can bet your life on it."
And when the cyclone turned the day into
night,
you held a flashlight and showed me the
safe way home.
You called for help on your cell phone.
You said you'd never leave me.
You said, "Believe me,
in times of trouble you will never be alone."
They said it wasn't such a bad situation.
It was beyond imagination.
I'm just glad to be alive—
and that is no exaggeration.
(CHORUS)

Reinvent the Wheel [Unit 8]

You've got your digi camera with the
Powershot,
four mega pixels and a memory slot.
You've got your e-mail and your Internet.
You send me pictures of your digi pet.
I got the digi dog and the digi cat,
the digi this and the digi that.
I hate to be the one to break the news,
but you're giving me the digi blues.
(CHORUS)
And you don't know
the way I really feel.
Why'd you have to go and
reinvent the wheel?
You've got your cordless phone and your
microwave,
and your Reflex Plus for the perfect shave.
It's super special, top of the line,
with the latest new, cutting-edge design.
You've got your SLR and your LCD,
your PS2 and your USB.
I've seen the future and it's pretty grim:
they've used up all the acronyms.
(CHORUS)
I keep waiting for a breakthrough
innovation:
something to help our poor communication.
Hey, where'd you get all of that high-tech
taste?
Your faith in progress is such a waste.
Your life may be state of the art,
but you don't understand the human heart.
(CHORUS)

Workbook

Joan Saslow ■ Allen Ascher

with Wendy Pratt Long

PEARSON
Longman

Cultural Literacy

TOPIC PREVIEW

 Look at the ads for four different English language programs.

Study Chicago English Program
Chicago, IL, USA

Study English in the Windy City!
- Intensive 3-week summer program
- Monday–Friday: English classes from 9:00A.M.–1:00P.M., with daily afternoon excursions
- Live in dorms with your classmates
- Weekends: group trips to destinations outside of the city

Call 1-800-STUDY CH to register or for more information.

GO CANADA LANGUAGE SCHOOL
Vancouver, Canada
Live in the city on the coast, with mountains just 1½ hours away!

- 3-, 6-, 9-, or 12-month programs are available.
- English classes are Monday–Wednesday from 9 to 12 or from 2 to 5.
- Thursday and Friday—You work in a real Canadian company to practice your language skills and get international business experience.
- Make your own living arrangements. You can get your own apartment or share one with a roommate. Choose the part of the city that's best for you.

Find us online at www.gocanadalanguageschool.ca.

Lingua Tech English Language School
Melbourne, Australia

Learn English Down Under!
- 1-year program begins each January
- Create your own schedule from a large selection of classes, including: English Conversation and Pronunciation, English Grammar (includes reading and writing), and Business English
- Live with a family and learn about life and culture in Australia

English Exchange, through DCU (Dublin City University)
Dublin, Ireland
Live and Learn in Europe!

- ◆ 1- and 2-semester programs available (fall and spring only)
- ◆ Exchange program with many universities around the world, so your classes count towards your college degree
- ◆ Take classes in your field of interest at DCU with Irish students
- ◆ Choose whether to live in a dorm or stay with a family

Now answer the questions and circle the supporting information in the ads.

1. Which program is best for a university student? _English Exchange_

2. Which program is best for a person who wants to work in an English-speaking company during their stay? _Lingua Tech_

3. Which program is best for someone with a limited amount of time? _Lingua_

4. Which program is best for someone who wants to take a variety of different English language classes? _Go Canada x Lingua_

2 ⟩ **WHAT ABOUT YOU?** Answer the questions in your <u>own</u> way.

1. Which of the four programs is best for you? _____

2. What do you like about that program? _____

   _____

3. Is there anything you don't like about that program? _____

   _____

3 ⟩ **Read the conversation. Answer the questions.**

Nicole: Hi, I'm Nicole Best. Nice to meet you.

Todd: Nice to meet you, too. I'm Todd Vernon. Do people usually call you Nicole, or do you prefer Nikki?

Nicole: At work I prefer Nicole, but all my friends call me Nikki.

Todd: You use first names in your office? That's great. My office is so formal. Everyone uses a title and their last name.

Nicole: I know what you mean. At my last job, everyone called me Miss Best, and that seemed really strange.

1. Are the people in Nicole's office on a first-name basis? _Nicole - Yes, they call her Nikki_

2. What do Todd's colleagues call him? _Nikki_

3. What would Todd prefer to be called? _Todd_

4. Is Nicole married? _No_

4 ⟩ **Match the correct response to each statement or question. Write the letter on the line.**

1. Nice to meet you. _c_

2. What is the custom here? _d_

3. How would you like to be addressed? _b_

4. Are most people on a first-name basis? _a_

a. Yes, they are.

b. I'd like to be called by my nickname.

c. Nice to meet you, too.

d. I'm not sure. It's probably best to watch what others do.

5 ⟩ **WHAT ABOUT YOU?** Answer the questions in your <u>own</u> way.

1. What do you prefer to be called by your family? _May_

2. What do you like to be called by your friends? _May_

3. What do you prefer to be called by your colleagues or classmates? _May_

LESSON 1

6 ⟩ **Put the conversation in the correct order. Write the number on the line.**

_1_ Hi! It's a great day, isn't it?

____ Thanks. You, too. Would it be rude to call you Joe?

____ It really is. Allow me to introduce myself. I'm Amanda Decker.

____ Absolutely not. Please do.

____ Great. And call me Amanda.

____ I'm Joe Hanson. It's nice to meet you.

7 **Match the correct response to each question. Write the letter on the line.**

1. He didn't know about that custom, did he? __d__ ✓

2. It's a great day to go to the beach, isn't it? __b__ ✓

3. You learned Japanese in school, didn't you? __f__ ✓

4. Mike will be here later, won't he? __a__ ✓

5. You're not from Turkey, are you? __c__ ✓

6. The program in Bali wasn't very successful, was it? __e__ ✓

a. Yes, he will.

b. Yes, it is.

c. No, I'm not.

d. No, he didn't.

e. No, it wasn't.

f. Yes, I did.

8 **Look at the picture. Answer each question with a short answer.**

1. It's very good weather today, isn't it? _Yes, it is._

2. It's not 2:30 yet, is it? _No, it isn't._ ✓

3. It's a good day to ride a bike, isn't it? _Yes, it is._ ✓

4. There isn't a lot of traffic, is there? _No, there isn't._ ✓

5. Yesterday wasn't Sunday, was it? _No, it wasn't._ ✓

6. The people haven't met before today, have they? _No, they haven't._ ✓

7. They're not cold, are they? _No they aren't._ ✓

8. The man plays tennis, doesn't he? _No he doesn't_ ✓

9. The woman is going to read, isn't she? _Yes, she is._ ✓

H.W

simple past

9 **Read the situations and complete the tag questions.**

1. You think your friend got a good grade on her science test.

   "She ___got___ a good grade on her science test, ___didn't she___?"

2. You see two people talking, but you don't think that they know each other.

   "They ___don't know___ each other, ___do they___?"

3. You're talking to your friend. You think he'll be late to the party tonight.

   "You ___do think he'll be___ late to the party tonight, ___don't you___?"
   are going to be ~~x~~ *aren't you*

4. When you get to class, you think your friend Diane hasn't gotten there yet.

   "Diane ___hasn't got___ here yet, ___has she___?"

5. You heard that your friend Bill was in a car accident yesterday, but you don't think that's true.

   "Bill ___wasn't___ in a car accident yesterday, ___was he___?"

6. You think that Dr. Jenkins doesn't like to be called by her first name.

   "Dr. Jenkins ___does likes___ to be called Kate, ___doesn't she___?" ✓
   doesn't likes   *does she* ✓

10 **CHALLENGE. Read the information about Allison McFarland. Then use the information on the form to write statements with tag questions.**

Name:	Allison McFarland
Preferred title:	Ms.
Date of birth:	October 27, 1985
Place of birth:	Hong Kong
Country of residence:	Canada
Occupation:	student

1. _You're Allison McFarland, aren't you?_____

2. _____

3. _____

4. _____

5. _____

6. _____

11 **WHAT ABOUT YOU? Which topics are appropriate for small talk in your country? Check yes or no. If you check no, then explain why the topic is not appropriate.**

	yes	no	
1. the weather	☐	☐	_____
2. what someone would like to be called	☐	☐	_____
3. how much money a person makes	☐	☐	_____
4. a person's work or studies	☐	☐	_____
5. someone's marital status	☐	☐	_____

LESSON 2

12 Read each sentence. Circle the letter of the sentence that has the same or similar meaning.

1. "You were in this class last term, weren't you?"

   a. I don't think you were in this class last term.   **b.** I think you were in this class before.

2. "You look familiar."

   a. I think I know you.   **b.** I've never met you before.

3. "I hadn't arrived here yet when the class began."

   a. I arrived here before the class began.   **b.** I arrived here after the class began.

H.W

13 Look at the facts about some famous people. Complete the sentences with the words in parentheses. Use the correct form of the past perfect and <u>already</u> or <u>not yet</u>.

> • Known around the world simply as Michelangelo, the artist was a legend by age 30.
>
> • Wolfgang Amadeus Mozart composed his first symphony before he was 5 years old. He wrote a number of sonatas, concertos, symphonies, religious works, and operas before he was 13.
>
> • When gymnast Nadia Comaneci was 14 years old, she arrived at the 1976 Olympic Games without hope of winning a medal. Then she amazed the world by receiving the first perfect score recorded in Olympic competition.
>
> • Tiger Woods won his first golf tournament at age 2—in the category of children ages 10 and under! He won his first international tournament at age 8.
>
> • Steven Spielberg made his first amateur film at age 12.
>
> • Joan of Arc was only 17 years old when she led the French army to a great victory over the English.

1. Michelangelo _had already become_ (become) a legend by the age of 30. ✓

2. Mozart _had already composed_ (compose) a symphony by age 5. ✓

3. By age 13, he _had already written_ (write) a large number of pieces. ✓

4. Nadia Comaneci _hadn't yet received_ (receive) a perfect score when she arrived at the ✓ 1976 Olympics.

5. Before he was 3, Tiger Woods _had already won_ (win) his first tournament. ✓

6. But when he was 7, he _hadn't yet won_ (win) an international tournament. ✓

7. Before he was 13, Steven Spielberg _had already made_ (make) a movie. ✓

8. When she was 15 years old, Joan of Arc _hadn't yet led_ (lead) the French army to a ✓ victory.

> Although Albert Einstein is now regarded as a genius, one of his teachers once described him as a slow thinker and a daydreamer. He was 4 years old before he ever spoke and 7 when he learned to read!
>
> **SOURCE:** www.answers.com

Look at Ken Klein's weekly planner. Then circle the letter of the answer that completes each sentence. Today is Sunday.

MONDAY

12:00 travel to Copenhagen
7:00 meet Jason Bailey for dinner

TUESDAY

8:30 have meeting with Computech
12:30 prepare client presentation

WEDNESDAY

9:00 fly to Brussels
1:30 meet Clark Sampson for lunch
4:00 give presentation to clients
7:30 take clients to dinner

THURSDAY

9:00 read TechServe report
1:00 have meeting with TechServe

FRIDAY

8:00 have meeting with Nelson Company
3:00 present results of Nelson Company
   meeting
8:30 fly home to London

SATURDAY   (SUNDAY) today

exercise in morning
at gym

relax all afternoon!

7:45 go to the
movies with Tania

had

1. By 5:00 P.M. on Monday, Ken _____ to Copenhagen.

   a. had already traveled   **b.** hadn't yet traveled

2. On Tuesday, Ken _____ Clark Sampson for lunch.

   a. had already met   **b.** hadn't yet met

3. On Wednesday evening, Ken _____ to Brussels.

   a. hadn't yet flown   **b.** had already flown

4. Ken _____ the results of the Nelson Company meeting at 2:00 on Friday.

   a. hadn't yet presented   **b.** had already presented

5. Ken _____ all week before he was able to relax on Saturday.

   a. had worked   **b.** hadn't worked

15 **Look at Ken Klein's weekly planner again. Complete the statements, using the past perfect and _already_ or _not yet_.**

1. By the time he flew to Brussels, Ken _had already had_ the meeting with Computech, but he _hadn't yet had_ the meeting with TechServe.

2. At 7:00 on Wednesday, he _____ the presentation to the clients, but he _____ the clients to dinner.

3. Ken _____ the TechServe report when he had the meeting with TechServe.

4. Ken _____ the meeting with Nelson Company when he had the meeting with TechServe.

5. By Saturday evening, Ken _____ at the gym.

6. At 6:30 on Saturday, Ken _____ to the movies with Tania.

WHAT ABOUT YOU? Complete the sentences in your <u>own</u> way.

1. When I left the house this morning, I had already _____.

2. At 12:00 today, I hadn't yet _____.

3. By the time I started to study English, I had already _____, but I hadn't yet

_____.

LESSON 3

H.W

17 **Cross out the word or phrase that has a different meaning from the others.**

1. offensive   very rude   ~~polite~~

✓ 2. customary   not allowed   taboo

✓ 3. impolite   ~~nice~~   rude

✓ 4. not usual   traditional   =   customary

✓ 5. etiquette   punctuality   manners

> **Did you know . . .**
>
> that etiquette and rules for behavior have a very long history? The first instructions for etiquette were written in the year 2400 B.C. by an Egyptian named Ptahhotep. His guide included advice about how to get along with others and how to advance in the world.

Source: www.canoe.ca

H.W

18 **Read the article about punctuality. Then check <u>true</u>, <u>false</u>, or <u>no information</u>, according to the article.**

RIGHT ON TIME

Everyone knows that different cultures have different ideas about punctuality. But one country—Ecuador—is trying something new.

A group called Citizens' Participation has found that being late costs the country about $724 million each year. They report that more than half of all public events, as well as many government appointments and social activities, begin late. The group is trying to make people aware of punctuality and reminding them to be on time. The government, including the Ecuadorian president, is supporting the effort.

Hundreds of Ecuadorian organizations and companies have signed agreements to be on time. Posters have been put up that remind people: "If you're late, someone else is waiting." One newspaper prints a list of government officials who arrive to events late.

The campaign has generally been well-received by the Ecuadorian people and it seems to be working. Many businesses have reported that more meetings are now beginning on time.

Source: www.economist.com

	true	false	no information
✓ 1. The country of Ecuador made more money because people were often late.	☐	☑	☐
✓ 2. Citizens' Participation doesn't think punctuality is very important.	☐	☑	☐
✓ 3. The government of Ecuador wants people to be on time.	☑	☐	☐
✓ 4. Signs and posters have been made to remind people to be punctual.	☑	☐	☐
✓ 5. Punctuality is more important now in Ecuador than in most other countries.	☐	☐	☑
✓ 6. Ecuadorians are on time (less) often than they used to be. *more*	☐	☑	☐

19 **WHAT ABOUT YOU?** How important is punctuality to <u>you</u> for each of the following events? Explain your answers.

	very important	somewhat important	not important	Why?
work or school				
dinner at a friend's house				
a meeting with a coworker				
a doctor's appointment				
a movie				

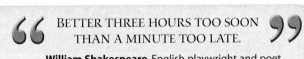

66 BETTER THREE HOURS TOO SOON THAN A MINUTE TOO LATE. 99

—**William Shakespeare**, English playwright and poet

LESSON 4

 20 Read the website and then circle the letter of the answer that best completes each sentence.

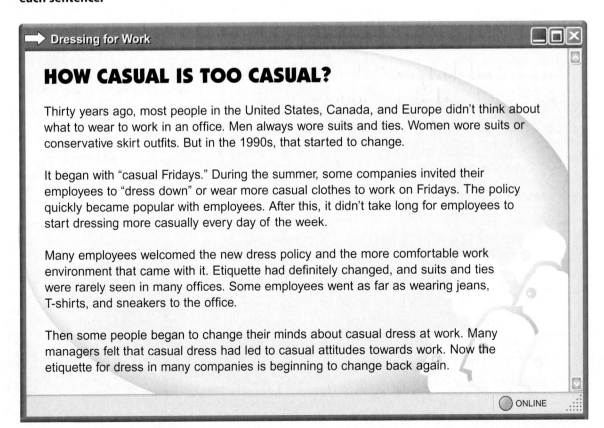

➡ Dressing for Work

HOW CASUAL IS TOO CASUAL?

Thirty years ago, most people in the United States, Canada, and Europe didn't think about what to wear to work in an office. Men always wore suits and ties. Women wore suits or conservative skirt outfits. But in the 1990s, that started to change.

It began with "casual Fridays." During the summer, some companies invited their employees to "dress down" or wear more casual clothes to work on Fridays. The policy quickly became popular with employees. After this, it didn't take long for employees to start dressing more casually every day of the week.

Many employees welcomed the new dress policy and the more comfortable work environment that came with it. Etiquette had definitely changed, and suits and ties were rarely seen in many offices. Some employees went as far as wearing jeans, T-shirts, and sneakers to the office.

Then some people began to change their minds about casual dress at work. Many managers felt that casual dress had led to casual attitudes towards work. Now the etiquette for dress in many companies is beginning to change back again.

○ ONLINE

SOURCE: www.careerknowhow.com

> **casual** (adjective):
> **1.** not caring; **2.** suitable for everyday use;
> **3.** without attention; **4.** not planned

1. Men used to wear _____ to work in an office.

    a. suits   **b.** conservative skirt outfits   **c.** jeans and ties

2. Casual Fridays started _____.

    a. about 30 years ago   **b.** in the summer   **c.** with women

3. Employees in most companies _____ the idea of causal Fridays.

    a. liked   **b.** didn't enjoy   **c.** didn't know about

4. Now many managers think that employees should _____.

    a. wear sneakers   **b.** not dress casually   **c.** work on casual Friday

5. Etiquette for dressing for work is once again becoming _____ in many companies.

    a. more casual   **b.** less professional   **c.** more professional

 21 WHAT ABOUT YOU? **Answer the questions in your <u>own</u> way.**

1. How has the etiquette for dressing changed in your country?

    _____

2. Is this change for the better?

    _____

22 **Read about Naomi's problem and give her advice about the etiquette and cultural changes in your country. Use ideas from the box or your own ideas.**

> I've been out of the country for over 15 years. Now I'm back, but so much has changed. I don't know what to do. Can you tell me about the changes in etiquette and culture?

> clothing customs
>
> dating customs
>
> forms of address
>
> male / female roles in the home
>
> male / female roles in the workplace
>
> musical tastes
>
> rules about formal behavior
>
> rules about punctuality
>
> table manners

GRAMMAR **BOOSTER**

A **Complete the following tag questions.**

1. We've met before, _____ we?

2. That movie wasn't very good, _____ it?

3. You _____ going to the party tonight, are you?

4. I'm going the right way to get downtown, _____ I?

5. Jane hasn't talked to Brian about the problem, _____ she?

6. The students call the teacher Mrs. Newton, _____ they?

B **Complete each sentence with the correct form of the words in parentheses.**
Use the present continuous or the simple present tense.

1. It _sounds_____ (sound) like they had a great vacation.

2. I _____ (have) English class every Tuesday at 5:30.

3. The children are hungry, so I _____ (make) them sandwiches.

4. The bus _____ (leave) at 3:00 on the weekends.

5. Dr. Angle always _____ (tell) her patients to exercise more.

6. Our boss _____ (go) to Cairo next Monday.

7. What _____ you _____ (do) tomorrow evening?

C **Complete each sentence in the e-mail with the present perfect or the present**
perfect continuous.

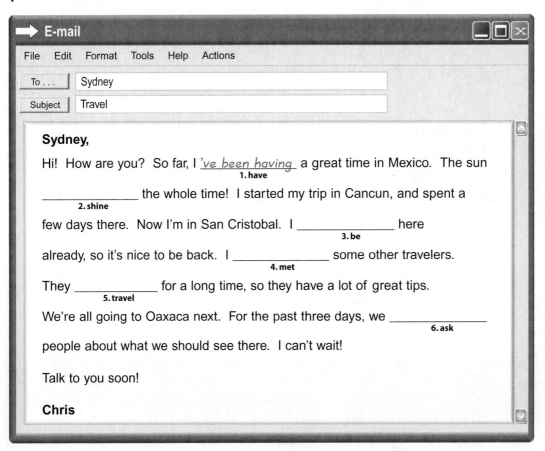

E-mail

File   Edit   Format   Tools   Help   Actions

To . . .   Sydney

Subject   Travel

Sydney,

Hi! How are you? So far, I _'ve been having_ a great time in Mexico. The sun
                                    1. have

_____ the whole time! I started my trip in Cancun, and spent a
        2. shine

few days there. Now I'm in San Cristobal. I _____ here
                                                        3. be

already, so it's nice to be back. I _____ some other travelers.
                                            4. met

They _____ for a long time, so they have a lot of great tips.
          5. travel

We're all going to Oaxaca next. For the past three days, we _____
                                                                        6. ask

people about what we should see there. I can't wait!

Talk to you soon!

Chris

WHAT ABOUT YOU? Answer the questions with your own information. Use the present perfect or the present perfect continuous and <u>for</u> or <u>since</u>.

1. How long have you been studying English?

   _____

2. How long have you lived in your house or apartment?

   _____

3. How long have you known your best friend?

   _____

4. How long have you been interested in _____?
   (Your own idea)

   _____

 Correct the verbs in the following sentences.

1. Sheila was studying in London when she ~~was meeting~~ *met* her boyfriend.

2. My family was going to Cairo last summer. It was a great trip!

3. I already seen that movie.

4. They have know her since 2003.

5. He didn't used to work there, but now he does.

6. I watched a movie when he called, but I didn't mind the interruption.

"Didn't anyone tell you about casual Friday, Johnson?"

Complete each sentence with the correct word or words, writing one letter per space. Then write all the letters in gray in order to find the answer to the joke. (Hint: The words are scrambled in the box.)

slaml katl	~~treiggens~~	oboat	trifs	tuqie
raley	sniveeffo	dusty draboa	stelit	rycastuom
labet nersman	plotiime	cleald		

1. <u>Hello</u> and <u>good morning</u> are two

   g r e e t i n g s .

2. Something that is __ __ __ __ [ ] is not

   allowed because it is very offensive.

3. To __ __ __ __ __   __ __ __ [ ] __ __

   is to live and take classes in a different country.

4. The boss likes to be __ __ __ __ __ [ ] by her first name.

5. Punctuality refers to the social rules about being

   [ ] __ __ __ __ and late.

6. You make __ __ __ __ __ __   [ ] __ __ __

   with someone to get to know him or her better.

7. Mr., Mrs., Miss, and Ms. are __ [ ] __ __ __ __ .

8. It's polite to be [ ] __ __ __ __ when someone is trying to study.

9. Another word for <u>usual</u> or <u>traditional</u> is __ [ ] __ __ __ __ __ __ .

10. __ __ __ __ [ ]   __ __ __ __ __ __ __ are rules for how to

    act when you eat.

11. In English, don't use a title with a person's __ __ __ __ [ ] name.

12. A rude or bad-mannered person is __ __ __ __ __ __ [ ] __ .

13. __ __ __ __ __ __ __ __ [ ] means <u>extremely impolite</u>.

Joke:
What kind of
ticket is accepted
at any event?

Nice to
meet you.

Answer: _g_ __ __ __

__ __ __ __ __ __ __ __ __

Answer: good etiquette

UNIT 2

Health Matters

TOPIC PREVIEW

 1 **What does each person want?** Write <u>dental care</u>, <u>eyewear</u>, <u>medication</u>, or <u>a vaccination</u> on the line.

> I want to make sure that I don't have a toothache while I'm traveling.

1. _____

> I have allergies. I need my doctor to write me a prescription before I go on vacation.

2. _____

> I want to be protected from illness and disease before I travel.

3. _____

> I'm going to the optician to get an extra pair of glasses before I go.

4. _____

2 **WHAT ABOUT YOU?** Which of the following health-related items do you take when you travel?

- ☐ extra prescription medication
- ☐ a prescription for extra medication
- ☐ non-prescription medication
- ☐ an extra pair of glasses or contact lenses
- ☐ a copy of your eyeglasses prescription
- ☐ special food
- ☐ exercise clothes or equipment
- ☐ the name and number of a doctor at your destination
- ☐ other: _____

PASSPORT

Before you travel internationally, check out the World Health Organization's website for updates on vaccination requirements, travel health risks, and precautions you can take: **www.who.int**

3 ▷ **Complete the conversations. Circle the letter of the correct answer.**

1. **A:** I hear you're from England.

   B: _____

       a. London.
       b. Yes, I am.
       c. I really appreciate it.

2. **A:** Thanks for fitting me in.

   B: _____

       a. Would you like me to make an. appointment for you?
       b. This tooth is killing me.
       c. Luckily, I had a cancellation.

3. **A:** _____

   B: Well, let's have a look.

       a. Can you recommend a dentist?
       b. Actually, there's one not far from here.
       c. My tooth hurts. I thought I should see a dentist right away.

4. **A:** This tooth is killing me.

   B: _____

       a. You should see a dentist as soon as possible.
       b. Can you recommend someone who speaks English?
       c. Thanks for fitting me in.

5. **A:** I need to see a doctor. I think it's an emergency.

   B: _____

       a. Thanks for fitting me in.
       b. OK, there's one not far from here.
       c. So, I hear you might be able to recommend a dentist.

Here are a few tips to maintain good dental health:

- You should brush your teeth at least twice a day, especially after meals.
- Brush your teeth for at least two minutes each time you brush. (Try timing yourself. Very few people actually brush for this long.)
- Brush gently with a soft toothbrush. Brushing too hard can hurt your teeth and gums.
- Don't forget to brush your tongue and the roof of your mouth.
- Change your toothbrush every three to four months.

Source: http://publicaffairs.uth.tmc.edu

LESSON 1

4 ▷ **Complete the conversation. Use the words and phrases from the box. You will not use all of the words and phrases.**

| an appointment | appreciate | business | could be here | must hurt | pain | a toothache |

Receptionist: Hello, Dr. Winters' office.

Alexander York: Hello. I'm calling because I'd like to make _____ to see
                       1.
        the dentist. I have _____.
                    2.

Receptionist: Are you in a lot of _____?
                              3.

Alexander York: Yes, my tooth is killing me.

Receptionist: Let me check the schedule . . . can you come in at 4:00? Luckily, I had
        a cancellation.

Alexander York: That's great. I _____ it.
                          4.

5 ▷ Now answer these questions about the conversation. Check yes, no, or no information.

	yes	no	no information
1. Does the receptionist need an appointment?	☐	☐	☐
2. Does Mr. York's tooth hurt?	☐	☐	☐
3. Is Mr. York from overseas?	☐	☐	☐
4. Can the dentist see Mr. York today?	☐	☐	☐

6 ▷ Circle the letter of the word or phrase that correctly completes each sentence.

1. My gums _____.

    a. are swollen   **b.** came out

2. The patient's filling _____.

    a. is broken   **b.** came out

3. His tooth really hurts. He _____ it.

    a. broke   **b.** lost

4. I think _____ is loose.

    a. my crown   **b.** my toothache

5. If you lose a _____, then you have a hole in your tooth.

    a. bridge   **b.** filling

7 ▷ Circle the word or words that correctly complete each sentence.

1. The dentist (may) / must be able to see you today, but I'm not sure.

2. Your gums are really swollen. You might / (must) be in a lot of pain.

3. Bill hates to miss class. He (must) / might be really sick if he's not here today.

4. We must / (might) go shopping this weekend. It depends on if we have time.

5. You lost a filling? That (must) / may really hurt!

6. The patient (might) / must need a new crown. The dentist will have to look at the tooth to be sure.

7. Susan (must) / may not meet us for dinner if she leaves work late.

8 ▷ Look at the pictures. Complete each sentence with must or must not to make a conclusion.

1. He ___must___ be getting a checkup.

2. He ___must___ be going on vacation.

3. She ___must not___ like the dark.

4. The dog ___must___ want to go swimming.

5. She ___must not___ have gloves with her.

9 **CHALLENGE. Rewrite each sentence using _may_, _might_, or _must_ with the correct form of _be able to_ or _have to_.**

1. Her toothache went away. She _might not have to_ go to the dentist.

2. Dr. Morris is very busy today. He _may/might not be able to_ see you.

3. I think my crown is loose. I _may/might have to_ get a new one.

4. If I leave work at 5 o'clock, I _might be able to_ get there by 5:30. It depends on how much traffic there is.

5. Mrs. Graham slept until 10 o'clock, took her dog for a walk, and then went shopping. She _may not be able to_ go to work today.

LESSON 2

10 **Write each word from the box in the correct column to make complete sentences.**

abdomen	~~chest~~	~~coughing~~	dizzy	hip	nauseous
ribs	short of breath	sneezing	vomiting	~~weak~~	wheezing

I have a pain in my . . .	I feel . . .	I've been . . .
chest	weak	coughing

11 **Write the word that matches each definition. Use the words from the box in Exercise 10.**

1. _____ part of the body between the neck and stomach

2. _____ not strong, without energy

3. _____ feeling that you're going to vomit

4. _____ making a noise by air suddenly coming out of the nose

5. _____ suddenly pushing air out of the throat with a short sound

6. _____ part of the body below the chest and above the legs

12 **Complete each sentence with a word from the box.**

a blood test	a checkup	an EKG	a shot	an X-ray

1. The nurse will take a sample of blood so _____ can be done.

2. The doctor will give you the medicine by giving you _____ in the arm.

3. The doctor is going to take _____ to look at the broken bone.

4. _____ records electrical signals from the heart's activity.

5. I'm going to the doctor for _____ to make sure that I'm healthy.

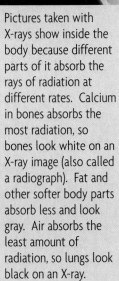

Pictures taken with X-rays show inside the body because different parts of it absorb the rays of radiation at different rates. Calcium in bones absorbs the most radiation, so bones look white on an X-ray image (also called a radiograph). Fat and other softer body parts absorb less and look gray. Air absorbs the least amount of radiation, so lungs look black on an X-ray.

Source: http://science.howstuffworks.com

13 **Who is speaking? Write <u>doctor</u>, <u>receptionist</u>, or <u>patient</u>. Some sentences have more than one possible answer.**

1. _____ "The doctor will be right with you."

2. _____ "I've been sneezing and coughing for three days."

3. _____ "I have an appointment with the doctor for a blood test."

4. _____ "Why don't you have a seat while you wait for the doctor?"

5. _____ "I'd like to make an appointment. I'm dizzy and nauseous."

6. _____ "Is anything bothering you today?"

7. _____ "Tell me about your symptoms."

8. _____ "Thanks for fitting me in."

9. _____ "Let's have a look."

14 **WHAT ABOUT YOU? Think about the last time you were sick. Fill in this patient information form from a doctor's office.**

Name: [_____]   Date of visit: __/__/__
                                     month day year

Date of your last checkup: __/__/__
                          month day year

Please check all of your symptoms:

1. Are you:
- ○ dizzy?
- ○ short of breath?
- ○ nauseous?
- ○ weak?

2. Do you have any pain in your:
- ○ abdomen?
- ○ ribs?
- ○ hips?
- ○ chest?
- ○ other: _____

3. Have you been:
- ○ wheezing?
- ○ coughing?
- ○ sneezing?
- ○ vomiting?

4. Please give a brief description of your illness:
_____
_____
_____
_____

"**An apple a day keeps the doctor away.**"

—This line comes from an old poem that was told to children to encourage them to eat healthy foods like fruits and vegetables. It's still a common saying today in English.

LESSON 3

15 **Match each type of medical treatment to the phrase that describes it.**

1. homeopathy ___
2. chiropractic ___
3. spiritual healing ___
4. acupuncture ___
5. herbal therapy ___
6. conventional medicine ___

a. is mostly used for treatment of pain and injuries

b. involves medicines being taken as teas

c. uses remedies that come only from natural sources

d. is based on science and study

e. uses the mind or religious faith to treat illness

f. involves needles being inserted at specific points on the body

16 WHAT ABOUT YOU? **What are some pros and cons of each type of treatment? Use your <u>own</u> ideas.**

	pros	cons
acupuncture	It can help you quit smoking. It's 5,000 years old, so it must work.	I don't like needles!
chiropractic		
conventional medicine		
herbal therapy		
homeopathy		
spiritual healing		

17 WHAT ABOUT YOU? **Answer the questions in your <u>own</u> way.**

1. Which medical treatments have you tried? _____

2. Which one(s) would you like to try or learn more about? Why?

_____

_____

18 **Read the website about a type of medical treatment. Then circle the letter of the answer that correctly completes each sentence.**

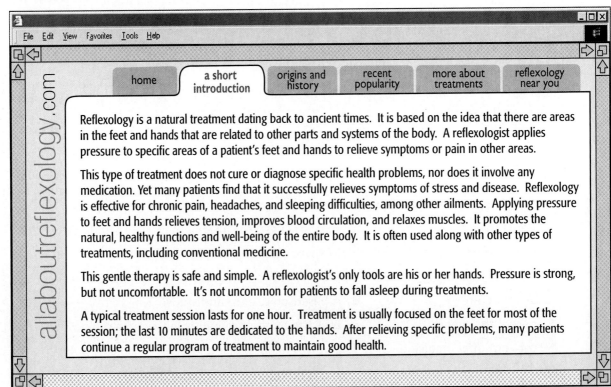

allaboutreflexology.com

| home | a short introduction | origins and history | recent popularity | more about treatments | reflexology near you |

Reflexology is a natural treatment dating back to ancient times. It is based on the idea that there are areas in the feet and hands that are related to other parts and systems of the body. A reflexologist applies pressure to specific areas of a patient's feet and hands to relieve symptoms or pain in other areas.

This type of treatment does not cure or diagnose specific health problems, nor does it involve any medication. Yet many patients find that it successfully relieves symptoms of stress and disease. Reflexology is effective for chronic pain, headaches, and sleeping difficulties, among other ailments. Applying pressure to feet and hands relieves tension, improves blood circulation, and relaxes muscles. It promotes the natural, healthy functions and well-being of the entire body. It is often used along with other types of treatments, including conventional medicine.

This gentle therapy is safe and simple. A reflexologist's only tools are his or her hands. Pressure is strong, but not uncomfortable. It's not uncommon for patients to fall asleep during treatments.

A typical treatment session lasts for one hour. Treatment is usually focused on the feet for most of the session; the last 10 minutes are dedicated to the hands. After relieving specific problems, many patients continue a regular program of treatment to maintain good health.

SOURCE: www.reflexology.org

1. A reflexologist is _____.

   a. person who provides reflexology treatment   b. a patient

   c. person who receives reflexology treatment   d. a doctor

2. The article <u>doesn't</u> mention that reflexology can relieve _____.

   a. headaches   b. problems with the feet

   c. tension   d. symptoms of disease

3. Reflexology _____ with other treatments.

   a. can be combined   b. is never combined

   c. isn't usually combined   d. might be combined in the future

4. In a typical session of reflexology, about _____ is spent on the feet.

   a. one hour   b. 50 minutes

   c. 10 minutes   d. half the time

5. The ideas behind reflexology are most similar to those of _____.

   a. conventional medicine   b. spiritual healing

   c. herbal therapy   d. acupuncture

19 **Complete the chart. Use the information from the website in Exercise 18 and page 20 of the Student's Book if necessary.**

Type of treatment	How it's similar to reflexology	How it's different from reflexology
homeopathy		
chiropractic		
acupuncture		

20 **WHAT ABOUT YOU? Which type of medical treatment do you think is best? Why?**

LESSON 4

 21 Suggest medications for the following symptoms. In some cases more than one type might be helpful. Explain why you think each choice is helpful.

symptom	medication	reason
1. sneezing	cold tablets, nasal spray, an antihistamine	They can all help reduce sneezing.
2. a toothache		
3. weakness		
4. coughing		
5. stomach problems		
6. a burn from hot oil		
7. red eyes		
8. an infection		

22 WHAT ABOUT YOU? How do you buy medications in your country? Which ones do you need a prescription for? Which ones can you buy without a prescription? Which are available both ways?

	prescription always needed	prescription not needed	some kinds require a prescription
antacids	☐	☐	☐
painkillers	☐	☐	☐
antibiotics	☐	☐	☐
vitamins	☐	☐	☐
cold tablets	☐	☐	☐
antihistamines	☐	☐	☐
other: _____	☐	☐	☐

> Drugs that can be bought without a prescription from a doctor are called over-the-counter drugs. You just go to the store and buy them at the counter. You don't have to go to the doctor first.

23 WHAT ABOUT YOU? Answer the questions in your <u>own</u> way.

1. What are some of the medications listed in Exercise 22 that you have taken?

_____

2. What is the normal dosage? _____

3. Do you need a prescription to get them? _____

4. What are some warnings or side effects of these medicines? _____

_____

GRAMMAR
BOOSTER

 Circle the word that correctly completes each sentence.

1. Some of the foods **must** / **may** contain peanuts. I'm not sure.

2. He hasn't slept in two days. He **might** / **must** be tired.

3. He's taking a lot of medication. He **may** / **must** be sick.

4. We **might** / **must** meet you later if we have time.

5. If Heather didn't eat any pizza, then she **must** / **may** not be feeling well. She loves pizza!

6. It **may** / **must** rain later today.

 Write one statement of possibility and one statement of probability for each item.

1. "I took a painkiller."

   You might have a headache.

   You must not feel well.

2. "She's been sneezing all day."

   _____

   _____

3. "That was very impolite!"

   _____

   _____

4. "What are the rules about punctuality in your country?"

   _____

   _____

5. "My feet are killing me!"

   _____

   _____

1 **WORD GAME.** **Look at the words below. How many new words can you make with the letters? Use only the letters in these words:**

> d e n t a l   e m e r g e n c y

men _____   _____   _____

real _____   _____   _____

_____   _____   _____

_____   _____   _____

_____   _____   _____

2 **JOKES FOR YOU!** **Unscramble the letters to find the answer to each joke.**

1. What kind of medical treatment is good for a person who doesn't want to leave the house?

   phemtooyah _____

2. What type of medication should you take if you're too hot?

   (2 words) _dolc sbattel_ _____

3. What kind of exams do vampires like?

   (2 words) _lodob setts_ _____

4. Why didn't the king feel good?

   He lost his _wronc_ _____!

Getting Things Done

TOPIC PREVIEW

1 Look at the business services offered at some office and print centers. Check the services that you have used.

☐ make black and white copies

☐ make color copies

☐ print documents

☐ print photos

☐ design documents

☐ make business cards

☐ other: _____

2 Look at the pictures. Which service does each person need? Write the correct service from the box.

copying	courier service	housecleaning	printing	tailoring

"Oh, no!"

"They need this package in Jakarta tomorrow."

"I'd like 100 more pages just like this."

1. _____

2. _____

3. _____

"I have the document on this CD, but I want to read it on paper."

"What a mess!"

4. _____

5. _____

3 Match the sentences with similar meanings. Draw a line.

1. I'm in a hurry.   **a.** I'll do it before I do anything else tomorrow.

2. I'm going to do a rush job.   **b.** I'll do this a.s.a.p.

3. I'll do it first thing in the morning. **c.** I don't want to take up more of your time.

4. I won't keep you then.   **d.** I have to go.

LESSON 1

4 Complete the conversation. Use the words from the box. You will not use all of the words.

appreciate	copy	enlarge	express	frame	print	urgent

Anna: Hello. Can I help you?

Greg: I hope so. This photo is too small. Can you _____ it?
                 1.

Anna: Absolutely.

Greg: I need this done right away. Do you have _____ service?
                     2.

Anna: Sure. When do you need it?

Greg: Well, can you do it in an hour? It's _____.
                    3.

Anna: Let me see . . . is 4:30 OK?

Greg: It's great. Thanks. I really _____ it.
                 4.

5 Circle the best answer to each question about the conversation above.

1. Who is Greg?

 a. a customer **b.** a patient   **c.** a worker at the store

2. What does Greg want?

 a. a copy   **b.** a larger photo **c.** a frame for the photo

3. What kind of service does the business offer?

 a. framing **b.** express   **c.** copying

6 Look at each pair of phrases. Circle the phrase that correctly describes a service.

1. dry-clean shoes   (repair shoes)

2. process film   frame film

3. dry-clean a dress   process a dress

4. shorten a picture   enlarge a picture

5. repair a package   deliver a package

6. print a report   print a suit

7. process a sign   print a sign

7 Complete each sentence with the passive causative.

1. We _will have the sign enlarged_ tomorrow because the printer is closed today.
   have / the sign / enlarge

2. Don't _have your film processed_ there. They've lost my film twice!
   have / your film / process

3. Can you please _get these pages copied_ before this afternoon's meeting?
   get / these pages / copy

4. Last week I _had my blouse dry-cleaned_, and now it looks like new.
   have / my blouse / dry-clean

5. Mr. Sutton needs to _have this package delivered_ to the Cairo office by Tuesday.
   have / this package / deliver

6. If you _get the photo enlarged_, the quality might not be very good.
   get / the photo / enlarge

7. Bill's pants were too long, but then yesterday he _had them shortened_.
   have / them / shorten

8. Sometime next week she _get her shoes repaired_.
   get / her shoes / repair

8 CHALLENGE. Correct the mistake in each sentence.

1. You can have the packages ~~delivering~~ _delivered_ to your home or office.

2. If you're getting dry-cleaned your suit, make sure you can pick it up tomorrow.

3. You can have your shoes ~~repair~~ _repaired_ for much less than it costs to buy a new pair.

4. We're having signs to ~~print~~ _printed_ to ~~announce~~ _announced_ the big event next week.

5. Where did you ~~got~~ _get_ your film from vacation processed?

6. You should get your skirt ~~shorten~~ _shortened_ so it fits perfectly.

7. I'd like to have ~~framed~~ this picture ~~so~~ framed so I can hang it up.

8. They didn't ~~had~~ _have_ the house cleaned yesterday.

9 WHAT ABOUT YOU? Which services do you use? Complete each sentence in your __own__ way. Use the passive causative.

1. I always have _my work clothes dry-cleaned_.

2. I've never had _____.

3. I have gotten _____.

4. Sometimes I get _____.

LESSON 2

10 ▸ **Put the conversation in order. Write the number on the line.**

_____ Have you taken your shoes there before?

_1_ Can you recommend a good shoe repair place to fix these shoes?

_____ Thanks.

_____ Of course. They do a great job.

_____ Why don't you have Sam's Shoe Repair do it?

11 ▸ **Circle the word or phrase that best completes each sentence.**

1. You can have someone **do** / does / to do that for you.

2. The lawyer will make them signed / **sign** / to sign the papers.

3. She got a service to clean / **cleaned** / clean her house before the party.

4. Why don't you get someone helped / **to help** / help you?

5. Mrs. Oliver always makes people to do / did / **do** whatever she wants.

6. Have someone else taken / to take / **take** care of that.

12 ▸ **Complete the paragraph with the correct form of the verbs.**

BEFORE:

My life used to be so crazy. I tried to do everything myself, and I never got anyone

_____ me. Then I realized that it's OK to have other people _____ a few things
1. help   **2. do**

for me. For example, now I make the kids _____ their rooms themselves. And I have my
                                           3. clean

husband _____ at the grocery store on his way home from work if I need something.
          4. stop

I've even gotten the kids _____ a little bit. It's not always the best food, but at least I
                          5. cook

don't have to do it! I've found that my life is much calmer when I have everyone _____
                                                                                  6. share

the responsibilities.

AFTER:

W26 UNIT 3

13 Read each pair of words. Write = if the words have the same or similar meanings, and ≠ if the words have different meanings.

1. efficient   _≠_   slow   5. reasonable   _____   priced fairly

2. honest   _____   not lying   6. reliable   _____   urgent

3. helpful   _____   smart   7. fast   _____   quick

4. professional   _____   busy

14 What kind of service is most important to each person? Use the words from the box.

We're looking for a business that will provide excellent service and results.

I need someone to explain things to me and give me advice.

I need someone who can use their time well to get the job done.

2. _____helpful_____ ✓

1. _____professional_____ ✓

efficient	fast	helpful
honest	professional	reasonable
reliable		

3. _____efficient_____ ✓

as

I need this printed a.s.a.p. It's urgent.

as soon
as posible

I don't want to pay too much.

I want someone who will tell me the truth.

I want to work with a business that does what they promise they're going to do.

7. _____fast_____ ✓

6. _____reasonable_____ ✓

5. _____honest_____ ✓

4. _____reliable_____ ✓

15 **WHAT ABOUT YOU?** Which adjectives from the box in Exercise 14 are most important to you for each of the following services? Why?

1. dry cleaning: _Professional. My appearance is very important, and if_
they don't do a good job, I won't look good.

2. housecleaning: _____

_____

3. package delivery: _____

_____

4. other: _____

_____

LESSON 3

 16 Read the article. Then check <u>true</u> or <u>false</u> for each statement.

"Dry" cleaning

Despite its name, dry cleaning is actually not a dry process. Clothes are washed in liquid chemicals, but without water (that's why the process became known as *dry cleaning*). But who came up with this idea, and how did it happen?

The invention of dry cleaning was an accident. In 1855, a Frenchman named Jean Baptiste Jolly made a discovery: a lamp filled with kerosene fell on a greasy cloth in his home (kerosene is a type of oil that burns well). When the kerosene dried, the cloth was cleaner where the liquid had been.

Based on this discovery, people began to use chemicals to clean clothes. But most of these chemicals, such as kerosene and gasoline, could easily catch on fire, so dry cleaning was very dangerous.

In the 1930s, people started to use a new chemical called *perchloroethylene*, or *perc* for short. This chemical didn't catch on fire easily, so it was much safer than the earlier ones. It is still used today by most dry cleaners.

SOURCE: http://science.howstuffworks.com

	true	false
1. No liquid is used in the dry cleaning process.	☐	☐
2. Jean Baptiste Jolly was trying to find a new way to clean clothes.	☐	☐
3. When kerosene got on the cloth in Jolly's home, the cloth caught on fire.	☐	☐
4. Kerosene can clean greasy cloth.	☐	☐
5. Dry cleaning was very dangerous because gasoline and kerosene catch on fire easily.	☐	☐
6. Perc doesn't burn as easily as kerosene and gasoline.	☐	☐
7. Perc isn't used in dry cleaning anymore.	☐	☐

17 Read the article again. Then answer the questions.

1. How is dry cleaning different from the way people normally wash their clothes at home?

_____

2. What chemicals did people use to dry-clean their clothes in the late 1800s?

_____

3. Why did people start using perc for dry cleaning?

_____

> **haute couture:** (French, literally *high* or *elegant sewing*) clothing that is custom-made and handmade from the highest quality materials.
>
> • Sometimes the phrase *haute couture* is used only to refer to French fashions; it also may refer to any unique, stylish design which is custom-made for wealthy and / or famous clients.
>
> • An *haute couture* dress can cost €10,000 or more.

SOURCE: http://fashion-era.com

18 Look at the completed customer survey. Then answer the questions about the customer's experience. Check <u>yes</u>, <u>no</u>, or <u>no information</u>.

Thank you for choosing **Sew Clean** for your tailoring and dry-cleaning needs. We want to know about your experience. Please take a moment to complete this survey and evaluate our quality of service.

	5 excellent	4 good	3 average	2 poor	1 unacceptable
Quality of work	⑤	4	3	2	1
Speed of service	5	④	3	2	1
Price of service	5	4	3	②	1
Knowledge of employees	⑤	4	3	2	1

Do you have any other comments? <u>The tailor knew what she was doing. She shortened my</u>
<u>pants perfectly. And they were ready on time. She told me that they would be finished</u>
<u>the next day, and they were!</u>

	yes	no	no information
1. Does the customer think that the business is efficient?	☐	☐	☐
2. Does the customer think that the business is professional?	☐	☐	☐
3. Does the customer think that the prices are reasonable?	☐	☐	☐
4. Does the customer think that the employees are helpful?	☐	☐	☐
5. Did the customer use the tailoring services?	☐	☐	☐
6. Does the customer think that the employees are reliable?	☐	☐	☐
7. Did the customer use the dry-cleaning services?	☐	☐	☐

19 Read and respond to the instant message. Describe the quality of the service and the workmanship.

Rudy425   ⬛ ⬜ ⊠

File   Edit   Actions   Tools   Help

rudy425: I'm new to the area, and would really like to know about the local services. Can you recommend any businesses?

you: _____

_____

_____

_____

_____

_____

👥 Invite   🖼 Send Files   📷 Webcam   🎤 Audio   🚀 Launch Site

LESSON 4

 20 Look at the plans for the party. Answer the questions.

Plans for Shannon's surprise party:

Mike: call Shannon's family to see who to invite
write down all the friends who we'll invite

Kayla: call friends and family to see when they are available
decide which day most people can come

Alan: visit Bryce Park and Shady Grove
decide which one is best for the party

Ryan: decide how to spend the money

Page: let everyone know about the party

Abby: buy balloons and "Happy Birthday" sign
get place ready for party

Samantha: call different restaurants and other places
get information and compare prices of food

Carrie: find someone to provide music

1. Who is going to pick a date? _____
2. Who is going to call some caterers? _____
3. Who is going to make the guest list? _____
4. Who is going to pick a place? _____
5. Who is going to hire a DJ? _____
6. Who is going to decorate the place? _____
7. Who is going to send out invitations? _____
8. Who is going to make a budget? _____

21 WHAT ABOUT YOU? Answer the questions in your <u>own</u> way.

1. Which step for planning a social event would you most like to do? Why?

_____

_____

2. Which step would you <u>least</u> like to do? Why?

_____

_____

22 Read the article. Then circle the letter of the correct answer to each question.

 **HOW TO ENJOY YOUR OWN PARTY**

Sometimes hosts are so busy planning a party that they don't enjoy themselves at the actual event. Here are some tips to help you relax and have fun!

Make lists of:

– everything you're going to clean

– how you'll decorate

– food that you'll serve

– stores you need to go to (grocery store, florist, party store, etc.)

– personal preparations (buy an outfit, get hair done, shower, etc.)

- Assign cleaning, cooking, decorating, and other responsibilities. Have your family and friends help, or hire someone.

- Decide which foods you can make before the day of the party. Have a caterer make everything else.

- Make a schedule for the day of the party. Include cleaning and decorating tasks. (It's always a good idea to leave more time than you think you'll really need.) Add personal preparations.

Now, follow the schedule you've made, and enjoy the party!

Source: http://entertaining.about.com

1. According to the article, you'll enjoy your own party more if you _____.

   a. plan for it well   **b.** look fabulous   **c.** serve delicious food

2. Make lists to help you _____.

   a. choose which foods to serve   **b.** make a hair appointment   **c.** plan

3. You should make food _____ the party.

   a. during   **b.** before the day of   **c.** on the day of

4. The article <u>doesn't</u> mention _____.

   a. getting people to help you   **b.** shopping   **c.** how to choose the menu

 23 WHAT ABOUT YOU? Answer the questions in your <u>own</u> way.

1. What do you think is most important at a party? Rate the details from 1 to 5, 1 being the most important, 5 being the least important.

   ____ music

   ____ food

   ____ decorations

   ____ place

   ____ other: _____

2. Explain why you think that _____ is the most important detail in party planning.

   _____

   _____

3. What are some reasons for having a party?

   _____   _____   _____

   _____   _____   _____

GRAMMAR BOOSTER

 A Read each sentence. Cross out the <u>by</u> phrase if it is not important.

1. I had my shirt's sleeves shortened by ~~someone~~.

2. The gallery always gets things framed by Colin's Frames.

3. We get our holiday cookies made by a professional bakery down the street.

4. They're having the package sent by Zipp's Delivery Service.

5. She got the kids' pictures taken by the person with the camera.

B Read each sentence. If the sentence is correct, write <u>C</u>. If the sentence is incorrect, write <u>I</u> and correct it.

1. Where do you get your film ~~to~~ develop_{ed}? _I_

2. I got the salesperson get me a different sweater from the back. ____

3. Parents should make their children brush their teeth every day. ____

4. Please get these pictures copying for me. ____

5. She makes her assistant stay late almost every day. ____

6. I'd love to get someone watch the children for a few hours a week. ____

C Look at the chart about what each child is permitted to do. Complete each item with information from the chart. Use <u>let</u>.

	go to bed late	eat a lot of sugar	stay home from school
Tina	✗	✔	✔
John	✔	✗	✗
Michael and Jim	✔	✔	✗

1. Tina's parents _don't let her go_ to bed late. But they _let her eat_ a lot of sugar.
And sometimes they _____ home from school.

2. John's mother _____ to bed late. But she _____ a lot of sugar.
And she _____ home from school either.

3. Michael and Jim's parents _____ to bed late. They also _____
a lot of sugar. But they _____ home from school.

D Read each statement. Give advice about what the person should or shouldn't permit. Use <u>let</u> or <u>don't let</u>.

1. "The kids are running all over the house."

(YOU) _Let them play outside. OR Don't let them climb on the furniture._

2. "My daughter broke a tooth on a piece of candy."

(YOU) _____

3. "I'm the only person who ever cleans our house."

(YOU) _____

4. "My little sister watches too much TV."

(YOU) _____

WHAT ABOUT YOU? **What was growing up like in your family? Complete each sentence in your <u>own</u> way. Use an object and the correct form of the verb.**

1. My parents had *me clean my room every week*   .

2. My parents didn't make *me and my brothers do laundry*   .

3. I used to make _____ .

4. I didn't let _____ .

5. My parents got _____ .

6. My parents let _____ .

7. My parents didn't let _____ .

F **Read each sentence and then answer the question.**

1. We had made some cookies for the kids.   Who made the cookies? *We did.*_____

2. Lisa had her parents send in the form.   Who sent in the form? _____

3. They had their friends move the furniture.   Who moved the furniture? _____

4. Jeff's boss, Brian, had canceled
   the meeting.   Who canceled the meeting? _____

5. We had talked to the clients about
   the problem.   Who talked about the problem? _____

6. Taylor had Steve take the messages
   for Christine.   Who took the messages? _____

JUST FOR FUN

 RIDDLES FOR YOU! **Answer the questions. Use the pictures for help.**

a. If a situation is urgent, when do you need to
   do something about it? _____

b. If you need a package delivered a.s.a.p., what can
   you ask the courier to do? _____

Answers: right away, hurry up

2 Complete the crossword puzzle. Use the clues below.

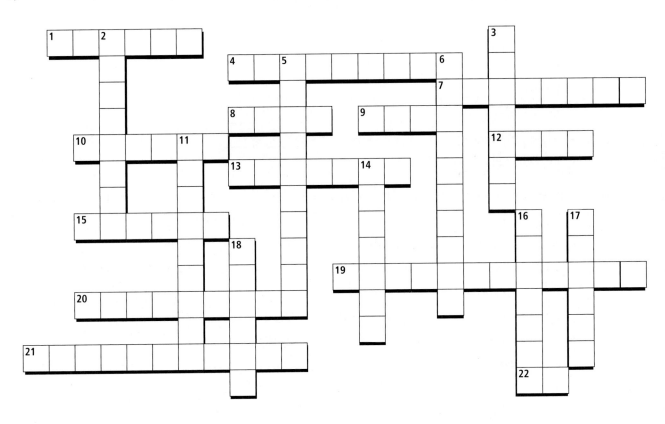

Across

1 Let's make a _____ so we know how we'll spend our money.

4 Have the package _____ to this address.

7 They're _____; you can trust them.

8 In Hong Kong you can get clothes that are made by _____.

9 Get your assistant to _____ the report. We need 100 of them.

10 You should have that picture professionally _____.

12 Do you have express service? I need this _____.

13 The _____ is responsible for preparing the food for the event.

15 When my shoe broke, I had the store _____ it.

19 A _____ business always does a good job.

20 It's cheap to get your film _____ at Stan's.

21 Have you sent out _____ to the guests yet?

22 The _____ is responsible for the music.

Down

2 Let's _____ the room to create a really fun, festive atmosphere.

3 A _____ person takes time to explain things to you.

5 Can I get this dress _____? It's too short for me.

6 I'd like to have these pants _____; they're so dirty!

11 The employees there are very _____; they do good work quickly.

14 Make the lab _____ the photo so we can see the details.

16 You can get signs _____ at that document processing center.

17 Be _____, and tell me the truth.

18 I had the dress _____-made, just for me.

UNIT 4

Life Choices

TOPIC PREVIEW

1 Complete the word webs. Write the professions on the lines.

builder	~~business owner~~	dentist	designer	doctor	~~family therapist~~
manager	marriage counselor	painter	scientist	song writer	tailor	teacher

business — business owner

science

social work — *family therapist*

arts

crafts

2 Do you know how to choose a career? Take this survey to find out how much you know. Check <u>true</u> or <u>false</u> next to each statement. Then read the article and check your answers.

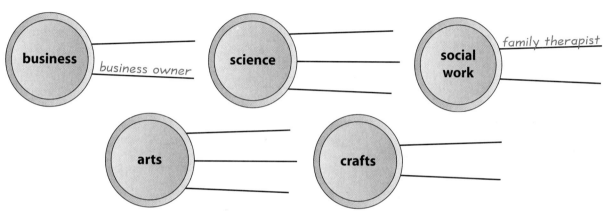

DO YOU KNOW HOW TO CHOOSE A CAREER?

true   false

1. It is always difficult to choose a career. ☐ ☐

2. A career counselor can't tell me what career is best for me. ☐ ☐

3. I might be able to make a living from my hobby. ☐ ☐

4. I should choose a career in a field that's expanding. Otherwise, it'll be too hard to find a job. ☐ ☐

5. Even after I begin a career, I can still change to another one. ☐ ☐

6. I can't learn about a job without really doing it. ☐ ☐

Some Tips on How to Choose a Career

Choosing a career is a very important decision. It can take a long time, and it usually isn't easy. You should think a lot about your likes, dislikes, and what's important to you.

- A career counselor can help you learn more about yourself and certain jobs to help you make a decision. But no one can actually make the decision for you.
- Think about jobs that involve activities you enjoy. It's possible to make a living from a hobby, whether it's selling your own paintings if you like to paint, or working at a camp if you enjoy being outdoors.
- Career experts predict which fields will grow in the future and offer lots of job opportunities.

But don't choose a career only because you think it'll be easy to find a job. In the long run, it's much more important to choose something that matches your interests and skills.

- It's okay to change your career. Many people change careers several times during their lives.
- There are lots of ways to learn about a job without necessarily having experience. Investigate careers online. Talk to people in that field. Try volunteering or working part time in the field.

SOURCE: http://careerplanning.about.com

W35

3 ▷ WHAT ABOUT YOU? Answer the questions with your <u>own</u> information.

1. Which field do you work in / plan to work in? _____

2. Why did you choose this field? _____

_____

4 ▷ WHAT ABOUT YOU?

a. **On a scale of 1–5, how important are the following qualities for you in a job? A 5 indicates that the quality is very important to you. A 1 indicates that the quality is <u>not</u> important to you.**

_____ make a lot of money   _____ work with people

_____ travel   _____ be able to work anywhere (from home, when

_____ work in a big company   traveling, etc.)

_____ have a flexible schedule   _____ have a lot of time to spend with my family

_____ be creative   _____ have a job that people think is important

_____ work outside

b. **Look at one of the qualities you gave a 5. Why is this quality important to you?**

_____

_____

5 ▷ Read each sentence. Then circle the letter of the sentence that has a similar meaning.

1. I got my head out of the clouds.

   a. I stopped dreaming.   b. I wasn't too late.

2. I got back on task.

   a. I started to do my work again.   b. I made a choice.

3. You can count on me.

   a. I'm reliable.   b. I stopped dreaming.

4. I wish I had gone to art school.

   a. I regret going to art school.   b. I regret not going to art school.

LESSON 1

6 ▷ Put the conversation in order. Write the number on the line.

____ No kidding! I thought you wanted to be a police officer.

____ What are you up to?

____ Great, thanks.

____ That's right. I was going to, but then I changed my mind.

_1_ Gerry! Long time no see!

____ Really? Why?

____ Well, I'm a lawyer now.

_9_ Well, my tastes changed.

____ Pat! How have you been?

7 **Read about these people's life changes. Then circle the letter of the answer that correctly completes each sentence.**

1. Fauja Singh started running again because _____.

   a. he was bored
   b. his son wanted him to
   c. he used to run with his wife

2. Fauja began running marathons when he was _____ years old.

   a. 89
   b. 53
   c. 42

3. Fauja runs faster than _____.

   a. all other marathon runners
   b. other runners his age
   c. no one

4. Fauja _____ his money _____.

   a. gives, to Adidas
   b. keeps, for his family
   c. shares, with other people

Fauja Singh

When his wife died, Fauja Singh left India to live with his son in Great Britain. He often felt bored and lonely with his new life, so he started running, a hobby he had given up 53 years earlier. In 2000 Singh participated in his first marathon at age 89, completing it in six hours and 54 minutes. He holds the world record for his age group. In 2004, Singh signed an advertising deal with the sports company Adidas. Singh gives the money he earns to charity. "After all," he says, "you can't take it with you."

SOURCE: www.nydailynews.com

5. Anna Robertson started to paint when she _____.

   a. moved to New York City
   b. was in her 70s
   c. needed money

6. Anna used to _____ before she started to _____.

   a. sew, paint
   b. paint, sew
   c. sell paintings, paint

7. Anna sold some of her paintings _____.

   a. to the Museum of Modern Art
   b. to an art collector
   c. to other American artists

In her 70s, Anna Mary Robertson Moses enjoyed sewing. But as she grew older, it became painful for her. So at age 75, Anna began to paint instead. She tried to sell a few of her paintings locally to make a little money. An art collector saw the paintings and bought them all. He was so impressed that he convinced the Museum of Modern Art in New York City to show some of her paintings. The next year, she had an exclusive show.

She became known as "Grandma Moses" and continued to paint until she died at the age of 101. In 26 years she produced over 1,600 paintings and became one of the best-known American artists in the world.

Joy Ride by Grandma Moses

SOURCE: www.tribuneindia.com

 Life is what happens to you / While you're busy making other plans

—**John Lennon,** British composer and musician from the song "Beautiful Boy," which he wrote for his son Sean

"Beautiful Boy" Words and Music by John Lennon

8 Complete each sentence with <u>was going to</u> or <u>were going to</u>.

1. We ___weren't going to___ (not) visit Robert, but then we changed our minds.

2. Everyone _____ find out the truth, sooner or later.

3. They _____ (not) see that movie, but it was the only one at 9:00.

4. _____ she _____ move to an apartment in the city?

5. Who _____ watch the children this evening?

6. Mr. Nan _____ make the announcement at today's meeting.

7. _____ (not) Charlie and Kim _____ get married last month?

8. You _____ talk to your boss about getting a raise, weren't you?

9. I thought I _____ (not) like the book, but I really enjoyed it.

10. People _____ start complaining if something wasn't done soon.

9 Circle the letter of the answer that correctly completes each sentence.

1. Did you think you _____ feel this way about the news?

   a. would   **b.** were going   **c.** weren't going

2. I thought we _____ to eat dinner inside since it's getting cold.

   a. aren't going   **b.** wouldn't   **c.** were going

3. No one knew that the product _____ such a success.

   a. would   **b.** was going to be   **c.** wasn't going to

4. Bob and Glenn _____ going to wait for us, were they?

   a. were   **b.** would   **c.** weren't

5. They always thought they _____ move someplace warmer, but they didn't.

   a. wouldn't   **b.** weren't going to   **c.** would

10 WHAT ABOUT YOU? What life changes have you made? Complete each sentence in your <u>own</u> way.

1. I was going to _move to sanfrancisco_, but _I drove to boston_

2. I never thought I would _have to take care children_ but _I have_.

3. A few years ago I thought I would _go to hawaiie_, but I didn't.

4. Five years ago I thought I would _be scientist_ at my age.

11 Match the sentences with similar meanings. Draw a line.

1. I changed my mind.   **a.** I don't like the same things anymore.

2. My tastes changed.   **b.** I convinced her not to do it.

3. I talked her out of it.   **c.** I decided to do something else.

4. It's hard to make a living.   **d.** I didn't meet the requirements.

5. I didn't pass the exam.   **e.** I can't make a lot of money.

LESSON 2

 12 Read the conversation. Answer the questions.

Jessica: I should have continued playing the guitar.

Joshua: Why do you say that?

Jessica: I love music. It makes me so happy. I might have been famous!

Joshua: Maybe. But you never know. You might not have liked the lifestyle of a musician.

> **66** I would rather regret the things that I have done than the things that I have not. **99**
> —**Lucille Ball**, American comedian

SOURCE: www.saidwhat.co.uk

1. Does Jessica still play the guitar? _____

2. Does she regret her decision? _____

3. Is Jessica famous? _____

4. Does Jessica have the lifestyle of a musician? _____

 13 Complete Stacy's thoughts. Circle the correct word.

Stacy

I can't believe what I did! Everyone **may / must** have laughed so hard when they heard about it—I'm sure of it. I **should / must** have taken Jason's good advice. If I had listened to him, I **would / wouldn't** have made such a fool of myself! And I **shouldn't / must** have left immediately, either. I **might / must** have made the situation better by staying there for a little while. I **must not / should not** have been thinking clearly. But I just had to leave. Everyone **should / must** have talked about it afterwards. I'm so embarrassed!

14 Read the completed paragraph in Exercise 13. Then check the box that answers each question.

1. Did Stacy take Jason's advice? ☐ yes ☐ no ☐ maybe

2. Did Stacy make a mistake? ☐ yes ☐ no ☐ probably

3. Did Stacy leave immediately? ☐ yes ☐ maybe ☐ probably

4. Did everyone talk about it afterwards? ☐ yes ☐ no ☐ probably

15 WHAT ABOUT YOU? Answer the questions in your <u>own</u> way.

1. What do you think Stacy may have done?

_____

2. What is one thing that you shouldn't have done (but you did)?

_____

3. What is one situation in which you could have done something differently?

_____

16 Read each sentence and question. Then check the box that answers the question.

1. "Someone might have heard us talking on the phone."

   Did anyone hear them talking?   ☐ yes   ☐ no   ☑ maybe

2. "Jen, you could have gone with Steve."

   Did Jen go with Steve?   ☐ yes   ☒ no   ☑ probably

3. "We should have invited Rita to come to dinner with us."

   Did they invite Rita?   ☐ yes   ☑ no   ☐ maybe

4. "I must have left my keys at home."

   she conclude that left keys at home

   Did she leave her keys at home?   ☑ yes   ☐ no   ☒ probably

5. "The kids shouldn't have watched that scary movie."

   Did the kids watch a scary movie?   ☑ yes   ☐ no   ☐ maybe

6. "Peter might not have talked to Jill yet."

   Did Peter talk to Jill yet?   ☐ yes   ☐ no   ☑ maybe

17 CHALLENGE. Complete the sentences with a perfect modal and the verb in parentheses. In some cases, more than one answer is possible.

1. I _shouldn't have left_ (leave) before I finished my work, but I did.

2. James __should have taken__ (take) the job offer, but he didn't.

3. Bethany __could have talked__ (talk) to Dave. I haven't talked to her yet,
   but she'll tell us tonight.   *could / might / may*

4. Kelly ____~~would~~ _must_ have got____ (get) stuck in traffic. I can't think of another
   reason for her to be late.

5. You __shouldn't have sold__ (sell) your car, but unfortunately, you did.

6. Harry __might have gotten__ (get) home already, but I doubt it.

7. We __couldn't have done__ (do) anything differently, could we?

> **❝** Nobody on his deathbed ever said, 'I wish I had spent more time at the office.' **❞**
>
> —**Paul Tsongas**, United States senator and presidential candidate

SOURCE: www.zona-pellucida.com

LESSON 3

18 Complete each sentence with a word from the box.

experience	knowledge	a skill	a talent

1. _____ is an ability that you are born with.

2. _____ is an ability that you learn.

3. _____ refers to the time a person has spent working at a job in the past.

4. _____ refers to the understanding of a certain subject.

19 **Read the conversation. Check the skill, ability, or qualification that each person has.**

Ms. Pitts: So we're looking at three candidates for this job: Simon Clark, Clayton Boyer, and Christina Nelson. Let's talk about their skills and experiences.

Ms. King: Well, I was impressed with Christina's leadership skills. She has a lot of leadership experience.

Mr. Warton: That's true, but she doesn't have knowledge of sales.

Ms. Pitts: But she seems to have common sense. She must be able to learn quickly.

Mr. Warton: Well, if we're looking for knowledge of sales, Simon Clark is the best choice. He's had 12 years of experience.

Ms. King: But what about other skills? Clayton speaks Spanish, French, and Portuguese.

Mr. Warton: Yes, and he has a lot of artistic ability, too.

Ms. King: But the ability to think logically is more important than artistic ability for this job. And Simon can definitely think logically.

Ms. Pitts: Okay, let's look at Simon again . . .

	Simon Clark	Clayton Boyer	Christina Nelson
1. good leadership skills			✔
2. common sense			
3. experience in sales			
4. good language skills			
5. artistic ability			
6. logical thinking ability			

20 **Read the circled job advertisement. Check the qualities that are important for the job.**

- [ ] artistic talent
- [ ] management skills
- [ ] good communication skills
- [ ] experience in a similar position
- [ ] organizational ability
- [ ] computer skills
- [ ] mathematical ability
- [ ] compassion
- [ ] common sense
- [ ] manual dexterity

stant
President of
ds someone
yday tasks.
n Excel,
Good
uired.
ful.
-555-6390.

tant to
nancial
ng group.
must have
and
3 years
e required.
0, ext. 3232.

ADMINISTRATIVE ASSISTANT TO DIRECTOR

This is an exciting opportunity for a talented individual. The successful candidate will work with high-level individuals in the company. Responsibilities include managing the director's calendar and commitments, managing special projects, serving as the director's representative to other offices and individuals, and supervising the administrative staff. This position requires 5+ years in a senior-level executive/administrative position. Experience and strong knowledge in a variety of computer software applications is also required. The successful candidate will be quick-thinking, flexible, and have common sense. He/She will have strong organizational skills and attention to detail. He/She should also have excellent oral and written communication, problem-solving and project-management skills. Apply online at http://www.jobs.sanbellcorp.com, Job #0009838.

Administra
Full-time
small com
to assist hi
Must be p
Word, Pov
phone etic
Good men
Fax resum

Administr
Marketing
Small, but
seeks moti
support bu
Successful
excellent
people ski
administra

21 WHAT ABOUT YOU? **Answer the questions in your <u>own</u> way.**

1. What is one of your talents? _____

2. What is one of your skills? _____

3. What do you have experience with? _____

4. What do you know a lot about? _____

LESSON 4

 22 Read the article. Then circle the letter of the answer that best completes each sentence.

A Big Life Decision

Work at the office or stay home with the kids? This is a question that many parents face. Here are a few ideas to consider as you decide what's best for you and your family:

What do you need to be happy? Would you benefit from "adult" time away from your children each day? Or is it your dream to spend every possible moment with your kids? How you manage your career and your family is a very personal decision. Think about what you really want. If you make a decision you're not happy with, you'll regret it.

Discuss the decision with all family members. Your choice will affect everyone in your home, so listen to everyone's needs and wants.

Finances, of course, will also be part of your decision. Can your family afford for you to quit your job? Would you be okay with a smaller house or an older car if it meant you could stay home with your kids?

Also, think about a compromise. It's becoming common for people with full-time jobs to work from home a few days a week. Consider working part-time or even starting a small business out of your home to be with your children more.

No matter what choice you make, reevaluate your decision periodically. As your family's needs change, your work situation might change, too.

SOURCE: http://content.monster.ca

1. This article is about _____.

   a. making a decision
   b. why it's important to stay home with your children
   c. changing careers

2. According to the article, everyone should _____.

   a. consider what makes them happy
   b. stay home to take care of their children
   c. do what their children prefer

3. Finances should be _____ consideration as you make your decision.

   a. the most important
   b. one
   c. the only

4. The article does <u>not</u> present _____ as an option to consider.

   a. working in an office
   b. working part-time
   c. hiring a babysitter

5. After you've made a decision, you _____ change your mind about your decision if your family's needs change.

   a. may
   b. should
   c. shouldn't

23 Read the article again. Then answer the questions.

1. Before you make a decision about whether to work at the office or stay home with the kids, who should you talk to? _____

   _____

2. What are some important things to consider before making the decision to work at an office or stay at home? _____

   _____

3. In addition to working full time at the office or staying home with the children, what other options do parents have? _____

   _____

24 Write a paragraph about someone who made a difficult work or life decision. Include information about their past plans, how their plans changed, and possible regrets. You may choose someone you know or someone famous.

25 Circle the letter of the best response to each sentence.

1. "I should have gone to school instead of taking this job."

    a. "You must have changed your mind."   b. "Well, you're still young."

2. "Why did you change your plans?"

    a. "My friends talked me out of it."   b. "You never know."

3. "I wish I had moved to another city when I had the chance."

    a. "Maybe it's not too late."   b. "You must have moved."

4. "I should have been an artist."

    a. "Well, it's hard to make a living that way."   b. "It could happen to anyone."

5. "I shouldn't have spent money on that sweater I bought last week. I regret my decision."

    a. "Maybe you would have hated it."   b. "Maybe it's not too late to take it back."

GRAMMAR BOOSTER

 A Answer each question with your <u>own</u> information. Use the correct form or tense for expressing the future. Write complete sentences.

1. "What will the weather be like tomorrow?"

    YOU *It'll be sunny and warm tomorrow.*

2. "What are you going to do this weekend?"

    YOU _____

3. "When do you leave for vacation?"

    YOU _____

4. "What will probably be your biggest expense next year?"

    YOU _____

5. "What time are you leaving your house tomorrow?"

    YOU _____

Read the conversations. Cross out the incorrect choice.

1. **A:** Do you want to go to the park later?

   B: Well, they say it **is going to rain / will rain / ~~rains~~** this afternoon.

2. **A:** My car broke down! How will I get to work? I guess I **could take / have to take / take** the bus.

   B: Don't worry. I **am going to take / will take / can take** you.

3. **A:** Do you want to go to the movies tomorrow night?

   B: I can't. I **am seeing / will see / am going to see** a play. You **could come / should come / are going to come** with me.

4. **A:** Let's go to Bloomfield's this weekend. I need a new pair of shoes.

   B: I don't know . . . Bloomfield's **is having / can have / will have** their big sale tomorrow. There **is / will be / might be** too many people there!

5. **A:** The cable's out again! That's it! I **am calling / call / am going to call** a repairman!

   B: Go ahead, but it **will take / takes / is taking** hours for him to get here on the weekend.

6. **A:** We need one hundred copies of this report by the end of the week. **Will you make / Can you make / Do you make** them tomorrow, Frank?

   B: I'm sorry. I **will be / am / can be** busy all day tomorrow.

Rewrite each sentence expressing regret about the past. Use the word(s) in parentheses.

1. I didn't go to college, and I regret that decision. (wish)

   I wish I had gone to college.

2. I ordered steak, but now I'm sorry that I did. (should)

   _____

3. Steve only borrowed two books from the library, but a few more would have been better. (ought to)

   _____

4. The couple went skiing for their honeymoon, but it was a bad choice. (wish)

   _____

5. Katie ate so many cookies that now she feels sick. (should)

   _____

JUST FOR FUN

1 **WORD SEARCH. Find and circle these words in the puzzle. Words can be across or down. Starting at the top left and moving left to right, write the remaining letters on the spaces below. Read the message.**

ability	career	change	choice	decision	field	job
knowledge	leadership	logical	regret	skill	talent	work

```
l  c  h  o  i  c  e  i  r  l
k  n  o  w  l  e  d  g  e  e
t  v  e  w  f  j  o  b  g  a
a  b  i  l  i  t  y  i  r  d
l  c  a  r  e  e  r  t  e  e
e  s  k  i  l  l  h  o  t  r
n  u  t  r  d  w  o  r  k  s
t  e  c  h  a  n  g  e  g  h
d  e  c  i  s  i  o  n  r  i
e  l  o  g  i  c  a  l  t  p
```

___ ___ ___   ___ ___ ___ ___ ___ ___ ___

___ ___ ___ ___ ___ ___ .

2 **TAKE A GUESS! Do you think these statements are <u>true</u> or <u>false</u>? After you finish, check your answers.**

	true	false
1. Most people change jobs on the average of 3 times in their lifetime.	☐	☐
2. Kenyan women work 35% longer than Kenyan men.	☐	☐
3. Half of all Czech and Slovak men work on farms.	☐	☐
4. Danish workers go on strike 150 times more than Germans.	☐	☐
5. Most men in Sweden are about 33 years old when they get married.	☐	☐
6. Most workers in Japan work about 40 hours per week.	☐	☐
7. In the United Kingdom, 10% of mothers stay home with their children.	☐	☐

SOURCE: www.nationmaster.com

Answers: 1. false. The average is closer to 12! 2. true. 3. false. Half of all Czech and Slovak men work in factories. 4. true. 5. true. 6. false. About 76% of the Japanese work force works more than 40 hours per week. 7. false. Nearly 55% of mothers in the United Kingdom with children under 6 years old stay home with their children.

Holidays and Traditions

TOPIC PREVIEW

 Read the newspaper ad for an event. Then check <u>true</u> or <u>false</u>.

Join us at the **Dexter Hotel** **on December 31 to welcome the New Year!**

Here's just some of what you'll enjoy:
- beginning at 7:00, a five-course dinner planned and prepared by world-famous chef Pierre Raynaud
- live dinner music performed by pianist Oscar Herman
- at 9:00, a two-hour concert starring the Sassies, one of the hottest new bands in the city
- at 11:00, popular hits and all your favorite dance songs played by DJ "Raging" Robin Collins from radio station WROC
- hats and horns passed out at 11:30
- a countdown to midnight by DJ "Raging" Robin
- a perfect view of the fireworks over the Charlton River

Tickets must be purchased in advance. Go online to www.dexterhotel.com to buy tickets or get more information.

---

	true	false
1. The ticket includes dinner.	☐	☐
2. Oscar Herman is a radio DJ.	☐	☐
3. The Sassies will perform until 11:00.	☐	☐
4. You need to bring your own hats and horns to this event.	☐	☐
5. You can view the fireworks on a large TV screen.	☐	☐

② **Choose an important holiday in your country. Using the ad above as a model, write an ad for a party for the local newspaper. Include the same type of information as the ad above.**

---

3 Complete the conversation. Use the words from the box.

| get together | mobbed | spectacular | takes place |

A: Wow, the airport is _____. Why are there so many people here?

1.

B: It's because it's almost Thanksgiving. It's an important holiday here in the U.S.

A: Really? What's the holiday for?

B: It started as a harvest celebration. It _____ every year on the fourth Thursday

2.
of November.

A: How do you celebrate it?

B: People usually _____ with their families. That's why there are so many people

3.

here. Oh, and the food is _____! This holiday is about families . . . and eating!

4.

LESSON 1

4 WHAT ABOUT YOU? Complete the conversation in your <u>own</u> way.

Visitor: Tell me about a holiday that you celebrate in your country.

YOU Well, one holiday is _____.

Visitor: What kind of holiday is it?

YOU It's a(n) _____ holiday that takes place in _____.

Visitor: How do you celebrate it?

YOU Well, in my family we usually _____.

Visitor: That sounds great!

5 Complete each sentence with <u>seasonal</u>, <u>historical</u>, or <u>religious</u>.

1. A _____ holiday is a celebration of a particular time of year.

2. On _____ holidays, people celebrate something that happened in the past.

3. A harvest festival is an example of a _____ holiday.

4. A _____ holiday is related to people's beliefs.

6 Write the correct word(s) after each verb to complete the ways to
commemorate a holiday. Use the words from the box. Then write some
examples of holidays when people in your country do each activity.

| costumes | cards | the dead | ~~someone well~~ | in a parade | a picnic | fireworks |

ways to commemorate a holiday	holidays in your country when people do this
1. wish *someone well*	*On New Year's Eve we say "Happy New Year!"*
2. wear	
3. march	
4. set off	
5. remember	
6. send	
7. have	

7 **Match each word with the correct definition. Use the words from the box.**

| a card | a costume | the dead | fireworks | a gift | a parade | a picnic |

1. _____: something that you give someone, especially to thank them or on a special occasion

2. _____: a public celebration when musical bands, brightly decorated vehicles, etc., move down the street

3. _____: clothes worn by someone to make them look like a different person, an animal, etc.

4. _____: colorful explosives that people burn when celebrating a special day

5. _____: people who have died

6. _____: a meal that is prepared at home and then taken outside to be eaten

7. _____: a written greeting, often with a picture on the front, that you send to people on special occasions

8 **Circle the word(s) that correctly complete the sentences. In some sentences, both choices are correct.**

1. Anyone **who / that** tries this dessert loves it.

2. The parties **that / who** they have are always so much fun.

3. The New Fire Ceremony was an Ancient Aztec celebration **that it / that** was celebrated every fifty-two years.

4. An emcee, or master of ceremonies, is a person **who acts / he acts** as the host at a formal occasion.

5. The gifts **that / who** we buy each other are usually pretty small.

6. A host is someone **that / who** invites a person to his or her home.

9 **Write the adjective clause that correctly completes each sentence. Use the clauses from the box.**

that is celebrated in Latin America	who enjoy being outside
who is invited to someone's home	that are celebrated with the whole family
that people send to one another	who David can't stop talking about

1. This is great holiday for people _____.

2. I love holidays _____.

3. It's a holiday _____.

4. A person _____ is called a guest.

5. The cards _____ are usually very colorful.

6. She's the woman _____.

LESSON 2

 10 **Complete the conversation. Circle the best response to each question or statement.**

Mitch: Do you mind if I ask you something?

Vanessa: Yes, of course. / **Of course not.**

Mitch: I'm not sure about the appropriate behavior here. When you go to someone's house for dinner, what should you bring?

Vanessa: **You should bring a small gift.** / You should bring the host.

Mitch: Absolutely perfect. / **Thanks.** It's a good thing I asked.

Gift-giving Etiquette

- In Japan, China, and Vietnam, it is not customary to open a gift in front of the person who gave it to you. The gift is set aside and opened later in private.
- In Russia, gifts for children are usually opened in private, while gifts for adults are usually opened in the presence of others.
- In Germany, you should avoid giving large or expensive gifts in private. The larger the gift, the more public the gift-giving should be.

Source: www.1worldglobalgifts.com

---

 11 **WHAT ABOUT YOU? What's appropriate? When two people go out to dinner, who should pay? Check the answer(s) that you agree with. Then explain your choice(s).**

☐ The person who invited the other should pay.

☐ The person who makes the most money should pay.

☐ The older person should always pay.

☐ Both people should split the check.

☐ They should flip a coin to see who pays.

☐ It depends.

☐ Other: _____

Explain your choice(s):

_____

_____

12 **Read each sentence. If the relative pronoun can be omitted, cross it out. If it can't be omitted, circle it.**

1. The dress ~~that~~ I wore to the party is in my closet.

2. Anyone (who) travels on that holiday should plan for delays.

3. The woman that you were talking with is a professional party planner.

4. The couple who we saw at the movies last night used to live in our building.

5. Ella is someone who always makes people feel good about themselves.

6. On Valentine's Day, I think about the people that I love.

7. It's great to meet someone who goes out of their way to help you.

8. What should a person who's invited to dinner take?

LESSON 3

 Read about how one holiday is celebrated in different countries. Then answer the questions.

CHILDREN'S DAY

Children's Day is celebrated in many countries, on different days, and in different ways.

Japan

Originally a holiday to celebrate only boys, Children's Day is May 5 in Japan. Families with sons often hang paper decorations and display figures that look like warriors, or fighters, because they hope their boys will grow up to be strong and healthy, like warriors. They also display carp decorations, since carp is a fish that symbolizes success in life.

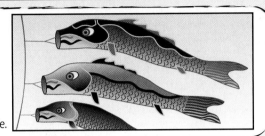

Korea

Celebrated on May 5, Children's Day is a national holiday in Korea. Many parents don't work and spend the day with their children. Families often visit parks, zoos, and movie theaters because they're free for children on this day. Parents traditionally give their children gifts and money.

India

Jawaharlal Nehru, the first prime minister of India, deeply loved children. His birthday, November 14, became Children's Day in India. Schools celebrate by having cultural programs and handing out treats and snacks. There are competitions and games of all kinds.

Turkey

Mustafa Kemal Ataturk, founder of the Turkish Republic, established April 23 as Children's Day in his country. People enjoy festivals and performances by children. Children replace the president, prime minister, members of the Grand National Assembly, and other officials for one day. They address children's and educational issues.

SOURCE: www.holidayinsights.com

1. In which country do children receive gifts on Children's Day? _____

2. In which country is Children's Day traditionally more important for boys than for girls? _____

3. In which country do children participate in government? _____

4. In which two countries was Children's Day started by a famous political leader?

   _____ _____

5. In which two countries is Children's Day celebrated on the same date?

   _____ _____

14 ▸ **WHAT ABOUT YOU? Write a paragraph about your favorite holiday. When is it?
How do you celebrate it? What traditions (such as special foods or clothing)
are part of this holiday? Is it religious, seasonal, or historic?**

LESSON 4

15 ▸ **Put the events below in the order in which they normally occur.**

_____ an engagement

_____ a reception

_____ a honeymoon

_____ a wedding

16 ▸ **Complete each sentence with the correct word(s). Use the words from the box.**

bride	ceremony	engagement	got engaged	groom
honeymoon	newlyweds	reception	wedding	

Neil and Carrie dated for three years before they _____. They were both so excited

1.

and announced their _____ immediately. They wanted everyone to know they were

2.

going to get married!

Today is the _____, which will have two parts. First is the _____, which is

3.   4.

the formal service that will make them legally married. Then comes the real celebration: At

the _____, everyone eats and dances for hours.

5.

Right now Carrie, the _____, is putting on her dress. She is so excited! Neil, the

6.

_____, is pretty excited, too, but he's also really nervous.

7.

Tomorrow morning the _____ are going to Tahiti for a seven-day _____.

8.   9.

After all the stress and excitement of the wedding, they'll need a vacation!

 The word <u>honeymoon</u> comes from an old Irish tradition. Newlyweds drank wine
made from honey for the first month (or moon) after being married. They believed
that by doing this, they would have a son within the first year of marriage.

SOURCE: www.irishcultureandcustoms.com

17 **Read the article. Then circle the letter of the word or phrase that best completes each sentence.**

Wedding Traditions: The Wedding Ring

At weddings in many parts of the world, brides and grooms give each other wedding rings. These rings remind them of the commitment they made to each other when they got married. They are also a sign to others that they are married.

No one knows for sure how this tradition started, but there is evidence that it began long ago in ancient Egypt. Coins at that time had a hole in the center. An Egyptian groom used to place a coin on his bride's finger to show that he would provide for and take care of her.

In many ancient cultures, including Egypt, the circle is a symbol of eternity. The wedding ring has come to symbolize endless love and commitment.

Wedding rings have almost always been worn on the fourth finger (the ancient Egyptians believed the vein of this finger went directly to the heart), but the hand it's worn on depends on where you live. In some cultures, people wear their rings on the left hand, and in others, they wear them on the right.

How the wedding ring fits is important. Some people think that the perfect fit of the rings represents a perfect fit between the couple: a tight ring can indicate jealousy, and a loose ring can show carelessness.

SOURCE: www.our-wedding-plans.co.uk

1. Rings are traditionally given _____.

   a. only in Egypt   **b.** during weddings   **c.** just to brides

2. Ancient Egyptian grooms gave their brides _____.

   a. money to buy a ring   **b.** money shaped like a ring   **c.** a ring for every finger

3. A wedding ring is a symbol of _____.

   a. eternity   **b.** a circle   **c.** love without end

4. Most people wear their wedding rings _____.

   a. on both hands   **b.** on the fourth finger   **c.** close to their hearts

5. A ring that fits too loosely symbolizes _____ to some people.

   a. a perfect fit   **b.** jealousy   **c.** not enough care

> King Edward IV of England, who reigned from 1461 to 1483, decided that the fourth finger of the left hand would be officially known as the "ring finger." This is still the most common name for that finger in English.
>
> **SOURCE:** www.wedding-rings.eu.com

18 **WHAT ABOUT YOU? Answer the questions in your own way.**

1. Do most people wear wedding rings in your country? _____

   If so, do they usually wear them on the left hand or the right? _____

2. What, if any, other symbols do people in your country use to show that they are married?

   _____

GRAMMAR BOOSTER

A ▸ **Match the incomplete sentences on the left with the phrases on the right.**
Write the letter of the correct phrase on the line.

1. The dentist _____ by my neighbor was really great.
2. We really liked the restaurant _____.
3. People _____ celebrate that holiday.
4. That holiday is fun for anyone _____.
5. The packages were from the employees _____ in the Tokyo office.
6. The package _____ came from Hong Kong.

a. who loves to celebrate
b. who work
c. that we received
d. who are very religious
e. that the book recommended
f. who was recommended

B ▸ **Rewrite each item as one sentence with a reciprocal pronoun.**

1. Adam sees Barb and Linus every day. Barb sees Linus every day, too.

   Adam, Barb, and Linus see one another every day.

2. Ms. Heidle waved at Ms. Cook, and Ms. Cook waved back at her.

   _____

3. Gerry meets Trish for lunch every day.

   _____

4. James, Erica, and Jessie were lost. All of them tried to find the others.

   _____

5. The employees buy gifts for the other people in the office.

   _____

C ▸ **WHAT ABOUT YOU? Complete each sentence in your <u>own</u> way. Use the correct reflexive pronoun and your <u>own</u> information.**

1. I really enjoyed _myself___ when I _went to San Francisco last month_.
2. In this class, we're proud of _____ when we _____.
3. I taught _____ to _____.
4. You need to take care of _____ when you _____.
5. My father introduced _____ to _____.
6. The woman gave _____ a gift because _____.

D Choose the phrase that correctly completes each sentence. Write the letter on the line.

A.

1. Don't talk _____.
2. Did you hurt _____?
3. You work _____ now, don't you?
4. You should be really proud _____.

    a. of yourself
    b. yourself
    c. to yourself
    d. for yourself

B.

1. She's feeling really sorry _____ right now.
2. She eats well and takes good care _____.
3. She always tells _____ that she's going to go back to school.
4. I think she should believe _____ more.

    a. of herself
    b. in herself
    c. for herself
    d. herself

E Complete each sentence with a phrase from the box.

by herself	by himself	by himself	by ourselves
by themselves	by yourself	each other	one another

1. Nobody went with Brian to the movies. He decided to go _____.
2. You can't dance the tango _____. You need a partner.
3. Young children often want to do things _____, even if it's difficult for them.
4. The players wished _____ good luck before the game.
5. Mrs. Jackson often works very late so her husband eats dinner _____.
6. We decided to do the work _____ instead of paying someone to help us.
7. Mrs. Kane and her daughter talk to _____ on the phone at least four times a week.
8. Sarah prefers to be _____ when she does her homework.

F Circle who or whom and complete the sentences in your own way.

1. _Mrs. Reilly_ is my neighbor (who)/ whom moved in ___three___ years ago.
2. People **who / whom** talk a lot can be very _____.
3. My friend **who / whom** lives in _____ is a really _____ person.
4. The people **who / whom** I met when I was in _____ were really _____.
5. _____ is a family friend **who / whom** I have known for a long time.
6. My friend _____ is someone **who / whom** I talk to almost every day.

JUST FOR
FUN

1 **Write a word for each category. Be creative!**

1. a holiday   _____
2. an adjective   _____
3. a place   _____
4. a person's name   _____
5. a time   _____
6. an action verb*   _____
7. a food   _____
8. a liquid   _____

9. an adjective   _____
10. a thing   _____
11. an action verb   _____
12. a number   _____
13. a holiday expression _____
14. an action verb   _____
15. an adjective   _____

**Now use the words you wrote above to complete the reading. It will probably
be a little crazy, since you chose the words without knowing what the reading
is about. That's OK—this is just for fun!**

Have you ever heard of _____? It's a / an _____ holiday that
                              1.   2.

many people celebrate in _____. According to my friend _____, this
                                3.   4.

is how they celebrate it there.

Everything starts at _____ in the morning. The first thing that people do
                            5.

is _____. Then it's time to eat. The most popular food on this holiday is
       6.

_____. And everyone drinks _____. If you're invited to someone's house
      7.   8.

for a meal, it's customary to take a / an _____ gift, such as a / an _____.
                                                9.   10.

After eating, it's time to _____. This is usually done with groups of about
                                  11.

_____ people. Everyone says _____ to each other. Then, the last tradition
      12.   13.

of the day is to _____. Everyone does it. What a / an _____ holiday!
                       14.   15.

Did You Know . . . ?
According to the *Guinness Book of World
Records*, the song "Happy Birthday to You" is
the most popular song in the English language.

SOURCE: www.tribuneindia.com

*This is a verb that shows action, such as <u>jump</u>, <u>play</u>, or <u>walk</u>.